CHRISTIANITY AND
THE JAPANESE

CHRISTIANITY
and the
JAPANESE

Brendan R. Branley, M.M.

MARYKNOLL PUBLICATIONS

Maryknoll, New York

266.2

B 734

PREFACE

This book is written from the point of view of a Catholic foreign missioner in Japan. It does not try to be an objective study of Christian foreign missions or of the contemporary Japanese religious scene, though it includes some treatment of both.

It attempts to describe Christian missionary work in Japan today as it encounters Japanese society and Japanese cultural values. No attempt will be made to cover Japanese culture in itself, but only those elements that help to form the typical Japanese attitude toward religion in general and Christianity in particular. Historical treatment has been kept to a minimum.

Nor is the description of Christian missionary work in Japan intended to be complete. Not only is there a failure to take the Protestant missionary effort into account, but even Catholic missionary efforts are examined only as influenced by and influencing the changing Japanese culture. A further limitation is the experience of the author which comprises the basic material for this book. The views reflected, then, are based on contact with people in Kyoto and nearby Otsu and in the cities of Muroran and Tomakomai in Hokkaido, where I have been engaged in direct missionary work. Again, scant historical treatment of the

71311

Japanese church is included; only the unavoidable facts necessary to understand the present.

Preaching the Gospel successfully depends on at least two factors. One is communication, the ability to identify your audience and to place yourself in an effective position to reach them. In this, as our account of missionary practice will show, there has been some success in Japan and some progress. The other factor is the Gospel message, which must be thoroughly translated into terms meaningful to the Japanese. We must remember always that the Gospel in this context includes not only teaching, but the whole Church, its organization, the community at worship, and its activities in the world.

It is the task of the missionary effort to understand the religious feelings of the present-day Japanese and to shape the Christian message and Christian Church so that it *reveals* Christianity to the Japanese instead of hiding or distorting it by a Western shape, as too often happens.

The book is organized simply into an introductory chapter and three sections. The introductory chapter deals with the role of the Christian mission in Japan, the possibility of Christianizing Japan, and the mission of Christianity in Japan to supply a spiritual vision.

The first section deals with religion and Japanese culture, showing first of all the Church's openness to cultures other than those it has known before and, secondly, examining Japanese religions to show the instinctive religious feelings of the average Japanese as developed from his contact with Shinto and Buddhism. The experience with these religions combined with traditional Japanese attitudes on unity and community form the cultural background to the Japanese reaction to organized religion today. Many of these attitudes, values, and emotions are incorporated into some of the "new religions" and contribute greatly to their currently successful growth.

An account of missionary practices forms the bulk of the second section. The Christian missionary effort has been directed primarily toward spreading the teachings of Christ and has tended to neglect the development of Japanese religious values within Christianity. This concentration on communications has helped to identify the more receptive audiences and to devise means of contacting them. The progress of missionary work is most noticeable in this area.

Missionaries have devoted most of their efforts to salesmanship, so to speak, and in meeting sales resistance, have continued to emphasize the development of better sales techniques. Although this cannot be neglected, it seems imperative that the mission effort be directed also toward redesigning or repackaging the product for the local market. The third section indicates some areas of possible development in making Christianity in Japan truly Japanese rather than Western. For this work, experimentation in liturgy and church organization is as important as development in theology, so that the men in the field, no less than the expert, have an essential part to play in evolving a natural form of Japanese Christianity.

TABLE OF CONTENTS

CHRISTIANITY AND THE JAPANESE

Introduction

THE ROLE OF RELIGION
IN MODERN JAPAN

Does Christianity have a mission in Japan?
Does it have a role in Japan's future development? In
order to answer these questions we will have to have
some answers to more fundamental questions. Has
religion the right to invade a different culture? Are
the Japanese perfectly content with the religions
they already have? Are they searching for a moral and
religious vision more adequate to the demands of the
modern world? We will try to discuss these questions
one by one.

Japan is a lonely island, separated from the rest of
the world by her watery boundaries and closed to outsiders through much of her history. As a result, Japanese culture has developed in an atmosphere of relative seclusion. The seclusion was rarely absolute,
but it is notorious that foreign influences throughout
her history, whether oriental or occidental, have become domesticated in Japan while becoming influential
or permanent. Mainland influences, like the introduction of the Chinese written language, have usually

undergone considerable alteration, being first fused with indigenous elements in order to survive their new climate. The same is true of Buddhism in Japan. Not only did Buddhism make adjustments for the Japanese people, but there was also some assimilation with the native Shinto religion in its efforts to make itself acceptable.

No more did the introduction of capitalism in the nineteenth century upset the previously paternalistic pattern of commercial organization. Even today the largest and most efficiently managed companies reflect paternalistic patterns which may appear incredible to Westerners. The postwar period saw enormous efforts on the part of the occupation forces to introduce a stable democratic political system into Japan, but few if any observers are led to believe that the former mechanics of Japanese political life have been erased in the process. They still operate within the new structure.

The historical changes in Japanese culture which are stimulated by outside forces have generally not deeply altered the Japanese people's intense consciousness of their identity as a separate people, different from all others. Their love of their land is a consciously deep attachment, frequently articulated from the time of the development of their mythology of the birth of the country, from which they are not separated as Japanese. The Shinto religion and several of the new religions preserve this tradition of uniqueness.

The element of uniqueness, consciously celebrated by many of the Japanese religions, has helped to form a strong national image and tends to evoke, in one form or other, a deep feeling, almost a quest, for a national mission. Religious symbolization of these feelings was important even in the militaristic expansion before and during World War II, when the war policies were pursued under the guise of manipulated Shinto religion. So too, the currently successful new religion Sōkagakkai shows a strong nationalistic tendency and devotes some of its energies to electing its own representatives to the National Diet.

What this religiously inspired or supported national consciousness seems to suggest is that there can be no separation of native Japanese religions from the Japanese people. "Conversion" to Christianity appears at first to be an abandonment of Japanese identity. This in turn suggests a theory of culture which holds that religions are a cultural expression of the religious instincts of a people, and that since religion is one of the central elements in a particular culture, a change of religion necessarily entails the destruction of that culture, a fate regarded by cultural purists with a horror that knows no bounds. Thus it would follow that Christianity and Japan are really related like oil and water and cannot come together without violence to one or the other.

The only answer to a theory is a fact. A central fact in evaluating religion in Japan today is the invasion of island Japan by the West in wave after wave of cultural shock over the past century. The impact of the West and Japan's consequent shift to a cosmopolitan culture, open to scientific thinking, has proved permanently injurious to the native Shinto and Buddhist religions. Shinto, as an expression of national consciousness, played an important role that everyone is aware of as late as World War II. But as a religion it rested on shaky ground. Myths which explained the divine origin only of Japan and the Japanese people to the exclusion of the rest of the world were unable to account for a Western civilization whose superiority was immediately recognized and whose discoveries were adopted. An appreciation of the uniqueness and superiority of the Japanese perdured, but it was no longer possible to dismiss the world outside. Japan may still be an island, but it is floating in a common sea.

Floyd Ross in a recent book *Shinto: The Way of Japan* feels that Shinto's lack of dependence on revealed dogma leaves it freer to enhance the human spirit, especially as it is more rooted in "feeling and tradition" than in "thinking and logic." Yet he confesses the necessity of "solid persistent thinking" for Shinto if it is to exercise this leadership. It is hard to see how Shinto can retain its feelings and traditions by switching over to the rationalistic approach to human guidance. Is this Shinto or a new religion? Further, it is difficult to see what a religion of national consciousness has to say about other peoples and countries.

Buddhism has received a more subtle but a more damaging blow. What seems to be an essential element of the Buddhist intuition of ultimate reality is that the real world is pure spirit. The apparent world of matter and change in which we are drowned is actually an evil one, a punishment for an imperfect spirit. What appears to be the world is ultimately unreality, a trap for the spirit, an illusion. The physical world is unworthy of our attention. If there is any mental attitude which is anathema to scientific thought and an obstacle to progress, it is this. Science, on which a nation's entrance into the modern world depends, is unalterably committed to the ultimate intelligibility of the universe. Without this previous, if unconscious, act of faith that the world is knowable, natural science is unthinkable. But the Buddhist perception of the world as a cloud of illusion, radically unintelligible, is in flat contradiction to this attitude.

In accordance with its own position, Buddhism is largely disinterested in society, unconcerned about the pattern of worldly life which must, inevitably, be saturated with imperfection. It is the duty of man to rise above this. To despise the organization of earthly society is not likely to endear modern man to one's own picture of the world. Social life, including politics, economics, education, and culture, constitutes the one area of existence about which most of our concerns hover. In the modern world, to express disinterest in social life is tantamount to turning one's back on humanity.

By these attitudes Buddhism has alienated the creative spirit of modern man, and it is difficult to imagine how Buddhism would be able to overcome this indifference while still remaining true to its nature. No one expects Buddhism to disappear overnight in Japan or anywhere else. But it seems inevitable that it will shrink in man's estimation as it has in that of the Japanese, have a decreasing influence on his life, cease to evoke his loyalty, and finally take its place among other unacceptable views of man's position which have been discredited and are no longer able to contribute anything to man's effort to achieve justice, peace, and happiness. Buddhism, to the Japanese, has lost its intellectual respectability, a loss as irretrievable as the loss of virtue to a Victorian gentlewoman.

The Japanese intellectual, whose experience with religion is principally with Shinto and Buddhism, is reluctant to consider religion anything but emotion or sentiment. One of the reasons is that he cannot conceive of what else it might be. In Japanese religions there was never a close association of religion with truth, historical, moral, or theological, and the coming of science to Japan only completed the separation— a suspicion confirmed. The Japanese will likely see all religions as subjective, totally unrelated to what we think of as truth.

Of the Zen fad in the West, there is actually little to say, for there is no great Zen fad in Japan. There is almost certainly less practice of Zen in Japan than there is talk about it in the West. There are, of course, monasteries where Zen is practiced, but the practice is not a popular one and its influence in Japan is almost completely historical. While a few Western intellectuals are looking East for a superior religion, many and perhaps most of the Japanese are willing to admit that Christianity is superior to Buddhism. This does not, however, mean a great deal in personal terms. For it by no means suggests that the speaker is interested in becoming a Christian, only that his judgment tells him it is a better religion; this conclusion does not affect his emotions, on which religious choice depends.

A less theoretical piece of evidence for the dissatisfaction of the Japanese with their traditional religions is the recurrent phenomena of the new religions. During the twentieth century as well as during a part of the nineteenth, these new religions, one after the other, have succeeded in promoting themselves as likely candidates to replace the ancient religions. They have usually captured the imagination of the public for rather short periods, much like a fad. For a time, each has held the attention of the nation. A generation ago it was Tenrikyo, currently it is Sōkagakkai, but there is no reason to suspect that this too will not sink into relative oblivion as have its predecessors.

More important, probably, than the outlook of Japanese religion on the world is the outlook of the Japanese on their religions. Although the Japanese have certainly been involved in the development of their religions and their religious practices, it does not automatically follow that they are satisfied with them or even that they are not ashamed of them. To appraise just how much the Japanese are attached to their historical religions and what influences these exert on Japanese life something more than a romantic theory of cultural integrity must be examined. According to this theory, the Japanese are necessarily deeply attached to their religion, whereas in fact all available evidence points to the contrary.

Traditionally, it has been the custom in Japan to count the number of adherents to a specific religion by counting only the heads of houses, and simply including all the family with him. In addition, since the Japanese were required to register at a Buddhist temple from the time of the suppression of Christianity in the seventeenth century, a family may be listed as Buddhist while actually having no other connection with Buddhism than using the temple graveyard for the deceased members of the family. In short, the religion of the family does not necessarily entail a personal belief in such a religion by members of the family. Lastly, nothing prevents a Japanese from being a member of the Buddhist religion and the Shinto religion at the same time. Statistics of religious membership in Japan must be taken with great caution. The total membership of all religions in Japan is 128 million, and this is out of a population of about 98 million, certainly a remarkable proportion.

There have been quite a number of sociological inquiries on the general religious situation in Japan. While the recent spectacular growth of Sōkagakkai has certainly made it out of date in at least one area, a survey made in 1955 indicated that in the large urban areas 90 percent admitted Buddhism as the family religion, whereas only 32 percent acknowledged Buddhism as their personal religion. Among these urban dwellers Shinto claimed only two-and-a-half percent of the population as followers, while Christianity and the newer religions each had two percent. A nationwide survey of the same year revealed similar proportions, though slightly fewer Buddhists, 30 percent, and more Shintoists, seven percent, probably because of the relative strength of Shinto in rural areas. The most significant result of these inquiries is that 61.3 percent of the population of the major cities had no religion at all, while the nationwide survey showed that 55 percent claimed no religion, and this despite the undemanding requirements for religious membership in Japan.

If anything, the younger generation only betrays an increased indifference. According to one inquiry, 84 percent of college students declared themselves without religious convictions, while in another inquiry 87 percent of non-Christian students of a Catholic high school were without religious beliefs. In spite of the probable inaccuracies of these inquiries, there seems little doubt that the traditional religions in Japan have little hold on the modern Japanese.

The Japanese intellectual is neither surprised nor dismayed at the prospect. He freely admits that Japanese religions are largely a question of emotion and sentiment and that syncretism of two or more religions is a common phenomenon in Japan. His verdict is frequently that religion is a matter of relativity, a view probably derived from those who regard each culture as an autonomous absolute. The Japanese intellectual's judgment seems to be that religion is largely irrelevant to life, and this judgment is apparently shared by most of his countrymen.

Most Japanese will admit that religion is "necessary," but this only means that they think it is necessary that there be such a thing as religion for those who want it and rely on it, not that they themselves feel a deep need of it. This degree of religious indifference is due to a number of factors, among which are the nature of religion in Japan, the history of Japanese religions, and the impact of the West.

First of all, religion does not occupy the same position in Japanese society as in the West, and we are prone to assume a greater similarity than there actually is. When a Westerner hears that the Japanese are Buddhists, he often has visions of devout congregations of Buddhists gathering weekly at the temples for worship and instructions or sermons. This is hardly the case. There is little regular group worship and most individual believers go to the temple only in times of personal difficulty, on the occasion of a family funeral, and to visit the tomb of their parents in the August festival of the dead. What regular religious worship there is consists mostly of a daily obeisance before the family altar by one member of the family. This simple act is certainly sufficient to constitute the individual a practicing Buddhist. There are, of course, special prayers one can have said at the temple for the departed, and there are sutras which can be recited by the devout person himself, as well as other practices of devotion depending on the individual sect. Yet none of these special devotions is widespread, and they tend to be a refuge in times of emotional disturbance, whether temporary or chronic.

Not only is worship sporadic and often mechanical, but there is little in the way of moral direction. Although there is a general Buddhist injunction of benevolence toward all living things, it rarely if ever undergoes any particular application. In general, it must be said that there is no intrusion of religion on the individual's behavior in daily life. For Shinto there is none at all. This is not said in criticism of Japanese religions but only to remind ourselves that such views of religion tend to make religion inapplicable to daily life and remote from the consciousness of the believer most of the time. Religion that is not bound up intimately with life fails to influence daily action and is easily subject to the charge of irrelevance.

Japanese religions have never placed great emphasis on religious teaching. There is no program of religious instruction for the children of Buddhist believers, nor are adults the object of a teaching program in the fundamentals of Buddhism or Shinto. In their Japanese forms, neither of these traditional religions is seriously concerned with providing an intellectual grasp of the religion for the believer. There is instead a dependence on ceremony and a practice of devotion which are less able to exert a continuing influence on conscious life than on intellectual appreciation.

The history of Japanese religions indicates that not only has teaching been neglected, but that the practice of Japanese religions has never been very intense or very widespread. It is difficult to be a devoutly practicing Shinto believer, for Shinto devotion consists largely in a loyalty to the divinity of the Japanese expressed through an exultant emotion of recognizing a spirit which guides the nation or the village. There are, to be sure, some myths of the celestial origin of the Japanese, but is hard to say how seriously these have ever been taken by the relatively small number of people who have known much about them. Devotion is confined mainly to the recognition of the spirit of the Japanese people and a willingness to serve it, and hence has found its strongest expression in times of war. It is naturally open to political machinations, especially that of promoting obedience to the government.

Unlike Japanese Shinto, Buddhism possesses a rich literature and in some countries evokes great devotion on the part of a great proportion of the people. But not in Japan. Buddhism was brought from China by a succession of Japanese who went there to study. Many Buddhist monasteries were founded in Japan for the dissemination of Buddhist teachings. To a great degree, Buddhism flowered in and around these monasteries. The imperial court was another center of Buddhism, which thus became a serious religious influence among many of the nobles. The golden age of Buddhism in Japan ended with the thirteenth century. It was then that the last great strongholds of Buddhism were established and there has been no impressive vitality since. The most important monasteries around Kyoto became nearly military orders, and when the capital was moved to Tokyo, no great Buddhist centers were established around the new capital. When Japan became unified in the sixteenth century, the military power of the Kyoto monasteries was broken and with it most of their influence. Little growth of Buddhism has been exhibited since. To this day the great Buddhist centers are those of this time or before: the great temples were all founded before the sixteenth century. The decline of the monasteries was followed by the decline of Buddhist teaching and Buddhist learning even among Buddhist monks. For centuries a thorough knowledge of Buddhist teaching has been the prerogative of a few.

A religion that owes its vitality to a monastic system can hardly fail to suffer when the monasteries undergo a serious decline, as they did in Japan. They have never recovered. Many people have seen pictures of Burmese Buddhist monks clad in saffron robes who roam the streets begging their meals. For many Burmese boys, this monastic discipline comprises a period of some years when they study and live in a Buddhist monastery before assuming their place in the world. In some places it is considered a normal process of training for every young man. Naturally these young men acquire an understanding and appreciation of their religion which prepares them to live a rather devout life even after their monastic training is completed. There is nothing of this kind in Japan, no mechanism by which Buddhist doctrine and spirit are communicated to the average person. Japanese Buddhism is not the popular religion it is in Burma and some other Asiatic countries.

What popularization was attempted even during the golden days was largely a matter of inviting people to witness a ceremony or the teaching of a three-word prayer that was repeated endlessly. This last was a deliberate attempt to spread Buddhism among the common people, and it was largely successful only at the price of spreading it thin.

Both statistical information and observation reinforce the impression that the great religions of Japan are unable to elicit a deep commitment from the Japanese people or inspire the activity of their lives. This leads us naturally to a consideration of a "spiritual vacuum" among the Japanese caused by a split between the creative life of the nation and a spiritual vision able to guide it.

Much has been written about the spiritual vacuum in modern Japan, especially since World War II, sometimes with the misleading assumption that the war itself produced this vacuum by destroying Shinto as the state religion. The situation is hardly that simple. Shinto is a religion without much ethical content beyond a powerful thrust for nationalism, which only assisted Japan's militarism. Imperialism is no less devoid of spiritual value because it grows in the shadow of a religion. Rather it seems that military aggression is itself symptomatic of a spiritual vacuum in a nation which can find no better goals to pursue. The spiritual vacuum in Japan is not due to the collapse of Shinto, which never did a great deal for spirituality since it does not have generous spiritual dimensions, but existed before and has been widely felt ever since Japan's contact with the West one hundred years ago.

Japan's contact with the West revealed to the Japanese that the world had passed them by. They suddenly found themselves dealing with people who knew more, were able to do more things, and were more wealthy and powerful. Their response was an enthusiastic but well-organized adaptation of Western methods of transportation, industry, management, education, and agencies of government, including the modern army and navy. Within the amazingly short period of forty years, Japan was so reorganized as to be capable of defeating Russia in a war, thus displaying her essential modernization. Japan had traveled from a feudal civilization to a modern one in one generation.

Before this change there presumably existed an equilibrium between the limits of social power and the spiritual values which inspired and informed this society. What happened was a dramatically sudden and gigantic expansion of social strength and control, without any increase in spiritual value, creating a whole layer of human activity and social control uninformed by spiritual content, thus creating the vacuum. For the tremendous power to manipulate man's life which was Japan's inheritance from the West did not enlarge the spiritual powers of the Japanese to direct the use of this power. Shinto and Buddhism, as already explained, do not possess the spiritual values necessary to supply meaningful goals for modern society. This is why the Japanese have had to invent, at a furious pace, new religions which are directed, however clumsily, toward filling this gap. This is why, too, the new religions are organized as societies and heavily oriented toward political action. These new religions, however, only reshuffle the Shinto and Buddhist doctrines, and however interested they are in the spiritual formation of the modern world, they have basically no more to say on the subject than their Shinto and Buddhist ancestors. The vacuum persists, only intensified by the growth and complexity of modern scientific and technical skills, which give increased ability to manage human life without the least indication of what to use it for.

It might be remarked that this type of problem is one with which Westerners themselves are well acquainted, that, in fact, it is a world problem which is not peculiar to Japan or to any one cultural area.

There is admittedly a great deal to this, but there is still a great difference between what we call the West, the remnant of medieval Christendom, and the countries, principally of Asia and Africa, which have until recently been outside this cultural tradition. For the countries we loosely categorize as composing the West, despite a certain amount of cultural fragmentation and the loss of a clearly unifying faith, still retain many subsidiary beliefs of the Greco-Roman, Judeo-Christian tradition, beliefs which are of critical value in harnessing and guiding the enormous social energies unleashed by the scientific revolution of thought. However little science is able to examine our commitments and however little our critical philosophies are capable of justifying them, what passes for Western culture is now held together by certain uncritically maintained commitments. Among these is an ideal of equal justice, based on a recognition of the essential value of the individual human being and his dignity. We are also committed to the defense of the freedom of conscience and the desirability of securing maximum protection of human dignity—spiritual and moral values which are not susceptible of measurement or external appraisal. Instead, they are usually regarded as absolutes. Although there has always been a certain lag in the realization of these goals in the new social structures made available by scientific advances, in every Western country most men, who may agree on little else, agree on this and accept these as goals of society, explicitly or implicitly.

This intuition of the individual human being as one of inestimable value, whose inalienable dignity

makes him an ultimate end in himself, is not really a
theory so much as a cultural tradition. Although
many mutually contradictory philosophies have been
evolved to substantiate it, this commitment does not
depend on any of them. Man's dignity, on which all
our other values depend, is not the conclusion of our
social philosophizing but the accepted basis for all
of it. So it is not entirely satisfying to attribute all this
to Rousseau or Locke or Mill, who merely supplied
this vision with social or political possibilities of realization and frames of expression. It is not even
accurate to attribute this commitment to Roman law,
which provided a legal means of guaranteeing it, or
to Greek experiments with democracy, which was
rather a theory, never achieving the rank of unquestioned cultural value which it enjoys among us.

The essential equality and dignity of man does not
depend on political arrangements but originally on
something much deeper, the perception of all men as
children of God. Begun in Judaism, it was extended
by Christianity to include all men. St. Paul's letter to
Philemon, in which he asked him to receive his run-
away slave Onesimus back "no longer as a slave, but
instead of a slave as a brother most dear," manifests a
perception of essential human value which centuries
of philosophizing have been powerless to increase.
The increasing secularization of this idea into legal,
political, and social forms has provided us with a
guide in cultural changes. In Western tradition it is
still this often unconscious outlook on man in society
that has determined our judgment about success or
failure in utilizing the recently discovered truths and

power which science has injected into society. In the ceaseless process of refining its legal, political, and social goals, which has occupied us for many centuries, the West has evolved cultural patterns for adjusting its basic commitment to human dignity to our other cultural values, such as individual self-assertion, in the changing circumstances of increased knowledge and power.

But while the West's difficulties in readjusting to an ever-changing world are partially assuaged by the guidance it receives from the traditional goals it has adopted, non-Western nations, without this tradition and without these goals, are necessarily without this guidance—thus the spiritual vacuum that is created when non-Western cultures accept Western science. The enormous expansion of technical knowledge is guided only by an inelastic system of values which is perhaps indifferent to human values and worldly goals, as is the case in Japan.

Although the problem of infusing spiritual values into new forms of society is one that is faced by any cosmopolitan culture, there is nevertheless this difference between the West and such cultures as Japan. We have a cultural commitment to the absoluteness of man's dignity, a spiritual value derived from Christianity, while a country like Japan has no such thing, and is helpless in an attempt to maintain spiritual values in the modern forms of society.

At the conclusion of World War II, the United States began a long series of experiments in transplanting democracy. The Japanese were the first subjects of this experiment. A constitution was written which embodies a democratic form of government, guaranteeing huge areas of human rights. Doubtless it was carefully explained that every adult had a right to an equal voice in the choice of government and a duty to see that it would be one which would respect the constitutionally declared human rights. The government elected by this process is still in power and will probably remain so until it makes a serious error, for economic success is pretty nearly the only thing keeping it there. There is little deep commitment either to human rights or the democratic process in Japan. The discrepancy is that we in the West are already deeply committed to individual dignity and human rights, and we are likely to cling to a democratic government, which we feel embodies these ideals in political form, through thick and thin, while the Japanese have no system of values which commit them to any serious consideration of individual dignity, human rights or, needless to say, the democratic process. Thus, while there is widespread but mild approval of the present system of government in Japan, there is no deep commitment and many are deeply unhappy with it. It is not easy to get something to grow without roots.

Westerners are sometimes oddly naïve about the knowledge and power which are the gift of the West to the non-Western world. Too often we think that, given a modest amount of human decency, it is a simple matter to turn this knowledge and power to unquestioned human benefit, while in fact, knowledge and power are no more oriented toward human benefit than toward tyranny, unfortunately often their fate. The results of science are indifferent to humanity and unless a culture adheres to a framework of spiritual values which guarantees their application to human benefit and judges their application, there is no control over them at all.

The West has been successful in dispensing the results of modern science, but has generally failed to communicate any means by which they can be harnessed for human benefit. It is not unusual to hear or read the work of Japanese intellectuals who complain that the West has sent them a Frankenstein's monster, a marvelous scientific invention which is not accompanied by any effective book of instructions. Japan does not possess a set of cultural values, a system of morality, or a code of ethics which is able to cope with this strange new being which has emerged from Western laboratories.

The general inability of non-Christian moralities to deal with modern civilization imported from the West is hardly contestable. The West has seemed to leave non-Westerners only unmitigated cupidity as a motivation in life. Slums of ugly dimension, angry workers, discontented students, baffled intellectuals, and aimless politicians have so often been the social effects of Western civilization. Problems which have taken us centuries to manage even partially, armed as we have been with an unquestioned commitment to human values, we dump into non-Western countries which have no adequate spiritual defense against abuses. We are in danger of making the non-Western world the spiritual trashcan of the West.

There is no denying the ability of Western civi-

lization to cripple any system of spiritual values and
ethics that previously existed in non-Western worlds.
The drastic alteration in the pattern of human life consequent upon the adoption of modern civilization
renders previous moralities useless. So the West, in-
tending, let us presume, to benefit non-Westerners,
destroys the existing system of human values without
replacing it with another. The material prosperity
which is the hoped-for result of modernization is frequently accompanied by a cultural and spiritual im-
poverishment.

The disruption of non-Western value systems by
the West is not, in fact, due to proselytism on the part
of a handful of missioners, but to the reverse, the failure of the West to proselytize enough, to give a system
of spiritual values and a code of morality able to preserve traditional values of a culture in the face of an
array of economic, educational, and scientific Western
forces which may otherwise destroy them all.

The building of a Western-style economy and industry is one of the first concerns of a country which is
joining the modern world. But there is no particular
reason why this must result in the freedom of the individual to pursue his own talents. It may as easily
mean the complete suppression of individual enterprise as otherwise, as Communism is there to remind
us. Even education can be utilized either to suppress
independent thought or to promote it. Only an
adopted system of spiritual and moral values that recognizes the dignity of man, his freedom, and his conscience can prevent such suppression.

If there is anything that seriously disturbs the Japanese in their general enjoyment of modern life it is their fear of the atomic bomb. Naturally, they have all the reasons. The destruction of Hiroshima and Nagasaki has left a deep and lasting impression on them, and is never far from their consciousness. Among the difficulties of the modern world, their experience has brought to the surface an open dread of science uncontrolled by any human consideration. For they, more than others, realize that the forces of modern science unrestrained by a system of moral commitment are perfectly capable of obliterating the human race. As a result, they experience this spiritual vacuum, regardless of television sets and other opiates which fail to convince them that they are not living in a house of cards.

And yet there are people who are astounded that the Church should have so little respect for Japanese culture that it actually sends missioners over there to teach that all men are children of God, that they must love their neighbor who is their brother wherever he may live, that he may not hate or despise nor be proud or covetous, but must be a peacemaker and merciful, as he hopes together with his brothers to be reunited with his heavenly Father, and all this sort of medieval superstition! They presume that the Japanese are satisfied to giggle at their native religions, which they know are perfectly helpless to guide their lives in the modern world, and to be condemned to live an aimless life that can expect no justice and mercy, with nothing to look forward to but bigger television screens, for which they should be duly thankful to us, their benefactors.

In reality, the spiritual vessels of Japanese religions have run dry. The forms of Japanese religion, Japanese religious psychology, emotion, and artistic expression, badly need the content of the Gospel to preserve them and fill them with spiritual values capable of inspiring life in the modern world.

Nor is it only the individual who searches in vain. The fate of the continual development of Japanese culture, the spiritual health of the nation, will depend on the success of Japan's search for her role in the world and for a spiritual ideal capable of leading her there.

The big question remaining is whether Japan can adopt Christianity without ceasing to be Japan, without surrendering the values of her culture, especially those developed by her religious history. Although a more thorough treatment of the Church's attitude will be presented in the following chapter, we should mention here that a union of Christian revelation and Japanese religious values does not endanger either of them.

To examine the possibilities for Japan of adopting Christianity while still retaining her cultural identity we must appreciate the relative cultural freedom of Christianity. Certain religions, like those in Japan, differ from Christianity in that they do not emphasize revealed truth. In a Japanese religion, weak in truth content, the emphasis is placed on the form, the way of entering into the spiritual world and the artistic means of expressing the presence of the spirit. As a result, such a religion in practice has very little commitment to truth or to an object of faith. Instead there is a strong commitment to cultural patterns of religious expression. When a believer in such a religion speaks of faith, he is normally attempting to describe a satisfying emotional state of accepting the ultimate spirituality of the world, above the aimlessness and harsh realities of everyday life. Essentially, it is a way of inducing and manifesting a sentiment rather than an acceptance and practice of a divine truth.

For this reason many religions, such as those of Japan, are in fact wedded to a particular culture, since they consist primarily of particular approaches to ultimate reality and particular expressions of spiritual presence. Of the identity of the ultimate reality and the way of life which is incumbent on a believer, such a religion has little or nothing to say.

But this cannot be said of Christianity. To a Christian and to those who in the West owe their attitude on religion to Christianity, religious faith is an individual's commitment to a religious teaching he sees as absolute. Christian faith specifically is the acceptance of the Word of God through His Son, Christ; belief in the direct revelation of the Creator of the universe and willingness to follow the way of Christ in one's life. As a result, Christianity is likely to differ from many other religions in that it is a response to revelation, the pursuit of an already accepted goal, rather than a search for ultimate meaning. The Christian is convinced that he has already been told the ultimate answers. His religious practice is a means of making them a reality within himself and in the world, rather than a means of discovering them.

Christianity is a religion of revelation in which neither particular forms of worship nor detailed laws of behavior form part of the divine revelation. Even though worship and behavior are revealed, the particulars and details are not, differentiating Christianity from religions which contain particular prescriptions such as are found in Leviticus or the Koran and which identify the religion as that of a particular culture with its own patterns of life.

In Christianity, religious faith is distinct from religious expression and, though religious faith is an absolute, there is great freedom of cultural expression of religious truth and emotion. Even though the sacraments are an integral part of Christianity, there is little specific commitment to a cultural form in which they must take place. The Mass, for example, has existed in a wide variety of cultural forms, each enclosing the same reality but in visibly different dress, in keeping with a particular culture. Church structures and architecture and the types of religious imagery which are the artistic expression of religion are, like the forms of prayer, a matter to be decided on by the Church for each different culture. It is not a matter of revelation or of faith, but of organized expression, subject both to diversity and to change.

Even Christian morality is not a body of legislation, but a moral inspiration which does not envisage details of life, which are peculiar to one cultural pattern of life and are subject to alteration even within the same culture. We have only to think of the Church's former uncompromising stand on usury to remind ourselves that any significant change in the pattern of human life necessarily involves a change in the law which regulates it.

Even though it can only exist in this world insofar as it finds cultural expression, the Church may express itself through any culture. In contrast to religions of nonrevelation, Christianity is not a manifestation of the religious psychology of a particular people, nor a way of looking for God or a way of listening to Him, but an acceptance of the revealed Word that is heard. And in contrast to non-Christian religions of revelation, Christianity is not committed to any particular cultural pattern of behavior, but only to following God's Word in one's life. Christianity is a religion that is culturally neutral and takes cognizance of cultural diversity, and this not by disinterest or toleration but by its very nature.

The Church, then, is not eager to deny the religious insights of different cultures such as the Japanese religious patterns of thought and emotion, for these can provide an approach to the God of revelation as well as a search for the mystery of the universe, a form of religious expression of God's presence in the sacraments as well as a testimony of longing. The Church is not determined to obliterate any religious forms of a specific culture except in the few instances where they are hopelessly debased or openly contradictory to the Gospel. Since the religious forms of Japanese religions are cultural expressions of religious psychology rather than specific commitments to a truth, the Church seeks to fill these forms with the content of the Word of God, which will illuminate the minds thus informed and guide their lives by the Gospel. Cultural autonomy is not necessarily threatened by Christianity. Nor has Japanese culture developed a strict pattern of religious commitment which would eliminate Christianity from consideration. It is true that Japanese culture entails certain ways of approaching religion and certain patterns of religious expression, but this does not commit the culture to any one religion in particular. Any religion which is not rigidly committed to a contradictory way of approach or form of expression could find cultural expression in Japan. In fact, at least since the fifth century, before which records are scarce, there never has been full religious unity in this land of undoubted cultural homogeneity. So Japanese culture is not necessarily tied to a particular religion. Both partners are free to enter the union.

part one:

Religion and Japanese Culture

Chapter I
THE CHURCH AND CULTURE

It may be hard to accept the assurance that either member of the proposed wedding is free and willing to enter into the union. The Church in Japan does not appear over-eager in wooing Japanese culture. We must try in the first place to see if the Church's intentions are honorable and if Her courting rests on solid principles. In a later chapter, we must see what traits of Japanese culture the Church might appeal to in order to get the best hearing for Her proposal.

It is no easy thing to express oneself clearly in terms of a new culture. Externals which are clear signs in one culture may be meaningless or misleading in another. So it would not be surprising if the Church had good intentions toward non-Western cultures but still was not very successful in expressing them visibly and understandably. Something like this seems to be the case.

Theoretically, the Church's policy in dealing with other cultures shows the best of intentions, but theory, unfortunately, is invisible. Even within the Church, there are problems of this kind. At the Second Vatican Council Archbishop Zoghby, Greek-Melchite patriarchal vicar in Egypt, objected to the Church's extending one local church, that of Rome, to the universal Church, thereby ignoring other cultures. "Eastern churches," he said, "found that they possessed a religious, theological, monastic, and disciplinary heritage which was different from that of the West." [1] In another speech Archbishop Zoghby gave an example of how the Eastern church's method of using authority to guide the Christian people had been forced to conform to the cultural pattern of Rome. The episcopal synods had been deprived of all real power, which was taken over by the Roman Curia. "To take Patriarchs, who by right are the presiding officers of their Synods, and make them secondary and minority members of a Congregation with authority to deal with the affairs of their own patriarchates is actually a condemnation of the synodal form of government." [2] The non-Western bishops frequently felt that they were without the power to make the necessary adaptations to their own cultures. "The Church," said Archbishop D'Souza of India, "as a living organism, must adapt herself to the times, and as long as the essentials remain intact, should not remain changeless forever." [3]

The difficulties and failures in putting theory into practice are one thing, but the official pronouncements of the Church reflected in the statements of recent popes and in the recent conciliar Constitution on the

[1] Elias Zoghby, "Eastern and Western Tradition in the One Church," in *Council Speeches of Vatican II*, edited by Hans Küng, Yves Congar, O.P., and Daniel O'Hanlon, S.J., Deus Book (Glen Rock, N.J.: Paulist Press, 1964), p. 51.
[2] Elias Zoghby, "The Eastern Churches and Bishops' Conferences," in *Council Speeches of Vatican II*, p. 127.
[3] Eugene D'Souza, "Bishops and the Roman Curia," in *Council Speeches of Vatican II*, p. 130.

Church indicate a thorough commitment to the acceptance of other cultures.

> The Catholic Church . . . is supranational by its very nature. . . . She cannot belong exclusively to this or that people, nor even more to one than to others. . . . She cannot be a stranger anywhere.[4]

> The right to existence, the right to respect from others and to one's good name, the right to one's own culture and national character . . . are exigencies of the law of nations, dictated by nature itself.[5]

> The Church . . . does not identify itself with any one culture, not even with European and Western civilization, although the history of the Church is closely intertwined with it; for the mission entrusted to the Church pertains chiefly to other matters, that is, to matters which are concerned with religion and the eternal salvation of men. The Church . . . is willing at all times to recognize, welcome, and even assimilate anything that redounds to the honor of the human mind and heart, whether or not it originates in parts of the world washed by the Mediterranean Sea, which, from the beginning of time, had been destined by God's Providence to be the cradle of the Church.[6]

---

[4] Pius XII, Christmas Message of 1945, in *The Unwearied Advocate: Public Addresses of Pope Pius XII*, Vol. 1, edited by Vincent A. Yzermans (St. Cloud, Minn.: Saint Cloud Bookshop, 1956), p. 66.

[5] Pius XII, Discourse of Dec. 6, 1953, "International Community and Religious Tolerance," to participants in the Fifth National Convention of the Union of Italian Catholic Jurists, in *The Pope Speaks*, Vol. 1 (First Quarter, 1954), p. 65.

[6] John XXIII, Address to Participants in the Second World Congress of Negro Writers and Artists, April 2, 1959; quoted by Pope John in his encyclical *Princeps Pastorum*, in *The Pope Speaks*, Vol. 6 (Spring 1960), p. 131.

Through her [the Church's] work, whatever good is in the minds and hearts of men, whatever good lies latent in the religious practices and cultures of diverse peoples, is not only saved from destruction but is also cleansed, raised up, and perfected unto the glory of God.[7]

Though it is clearly the intention of the Church to show the utmost respect for cultures new to Her experience, practice shows that there is enormous difficulty in finding a visible expression of this, or even in finding an acceptable explanation of what "visible expression" means in practice. Gustav Voss in an article "Missionary Accommodation" refers to the "garb" of the Church.

The garb [of the Church] comprises all the other features that make up the external appearance of the Church, as for instance . . . the means and methods of Christian instruction, various institutions of social work and Christian charity, nonliturgical religious celebrations and popular devotions, ecclesiastical art and architecture, and certain popular customs and civil institutions that make up part and parcel of the life of the individual in his concrete circumstances.[8]

But this metaphor seems to place undue stress on externals, which might be interpreted to mean that the Church's accommodation to culture is somewhat superficial. It seems that the Church's acceptance of a culture should be more likened to a body than to a "garb."

[7] Constitution on the Church (Washington, D.C.; National Catholic Welfare Conference, 1965), No. 17.
[8] Gustav Voss, S.J., *Missionary Accommodation,* pamphlet, Missionary Academia Study, Vol. 4, No. 2 (New York: America Press, October 1946), p. 39.

Perhaps better than this would be the image of the Church becoming a new human person in a new culture, since its "accommodation" should include all that is contributed by human life and thought. What is important is that the Church manifest its nature fully as embodying Christ, the light of all the peoples. This seems to be actually closer to the Church's intentions toward culture as most recently expressed in the opening words of the Constitution on the Church of Vatican II:

> Christ is the Light of nations. Because this is so, this Sacred Synod gathered together in the Holy Spirit eagerly desires, by proclaiming the Gospel to every creature, to bring the light of Christ to all men, a light brightly visible on the countenance of the Church. Since the Church is in Christ like a sacrament or as a sign and instrument both of a very closely knit union with God and of the unity of the whole human race, it desires now to unfold more fully to the faithful of the Church and to the whole world its own inner nature and universal mission.[9]

Theory, as we have seen, remains invisible except insofar as it finds its way into the tangible reality which is the Church. We will next try to understand how far the Church has succeeded in accepting all of the human contributions of different cultures to the Church, or to put it differently, how much the Church's development has been influenced by different cultures. Throughout this brief, simple account we are interested only in seeing how freely the Church has used

[9] Constitution on the Church (Washington, D.C.: National Catholic Welfare Conference, 1965), No. 1.

the cultural traditions of the peoples she has found Herself among.

Though it may seem absurd to say so, Christ Himself was the first foreign missioner, whose Incarnation involved not only His own human nature but a specific culture as well, including an expression of His message in terms native to His Jewish people. And just as God could not become man without becoming a man of a particular culture—a Palestinian Jew of the Roman Empire—so the Church cannot exist without being a church of a particular culture. When Christ preached and lived His Gospel, He inevitably "incarnated" His message in terms of the Jewish culture of which He was a part.

The distance between the simplicity of the parables and the elaborateness of later theologies is not due, as some reformers have believed, to a betrayal of the Gospel, but to the distance between the Jewish culture of Christ's time and the complexity of later cultures.

The Epistles of St. Paul and the writings of St. John, for example, are not the "perversion" of the Gospel of which some Scripture scholars have accused them. St. Paul left the confines of the Hebrew culture for the larger cultural world of Hellenism and, in his attempts to evangelize it, was forced to recast the Church and Her message in terms of that Hellenic culture, with the distinctly abstract mental habits of the Greek-trained mind.

The Church became incarnate in the Latin world of the West partly through the use of Latin forms of organization for the guidance of Christian life, such as the diocese and Western monasticism, which fit its mentality and tradition so well. The Eastern church relied more on the personality and traditional position of its leaders to accomplish the same ends. This divergence is not wrong; on the contrary, it merely testifies to the divergence of cultures. Finally, such differences are inevitable and rightly so, for the Church cannot be true to itself unless it is true to each culture in which it finds itself.

Later ages saw the flowering of the Byzantine culture in the East and the medieval culture in the West. But as East and West drew farther apart in keeping with their now separately developing cultures, they lost the ability to communicate with each other effectively. While the Byzantine church was heavily dependent upon ancient traditions and its close union with the state, the medieval church depended increasingly on law as a means of protecting itself from state interference. In its attempt to draw the Eastern church firmly into its sphere of purely ecclesiastical rule, the medieval church ignored the culture in which the Byzantine church was incarnated. This failure of understanding was certainly one of the causes of the schism between the churches of the East and the West.

The tragedy of this schism did not, unfortunately, bring with it any appreciation of the real cause. So that as the medieval era drew to a close, there was an increasing centralization of the Latin church, and an increased insistence that all matters of Church concern be finally deliberated in Rome, where the Roman naturally judged all matters from the point of

view of his own culture. When the Reformation occurred there were many factors in operation, but one
was certainly the divergence of cultural growth that
had occurred in the late Middle Ages. England and
Germany were rapidly developing their own cultures
and were no longer simply borderlands of a decaying
Roman Empire.

In failing to recognize that it was dealing with
separately developing cultures, the Church failed to
incarnate itself fully within them. It became more and
more obvious that the Roman model was no longer
completely expressive of the Gospel in terms of English or Germanic culture. Many Roman customs were
exposed as quite foreign to the thought and way of
life of the people, so that the human form of the
Church, foreign to the northerners and not fully able
to express its divine nature to these people, was an
easy target for the Reformers. The permanence of
the Reform owed much of its success to a greater
fidelity to the culture of the people.

Scholastic theology, for one thing, had fallen
among thieves and, discredited in the view of the
leading minds of the age, was no longer able to
express the teachings of Christ. The Reformers felt almost driven to a direct reliance on the Bible, however
problematic interpretation might prove.

The Reformation was a movement that brought
about great innovations in the liturgy and these probably supplied greater popular support than did the
theological differences, which could scarcely be
grasped by the average person. The majesty of Roman
ceremony, deeply expressive of God's majesty to

Romans, appeared more as worldly pomp within northern cultures. In order to provide worship in a natural form, the Reformers showed the opposite tendency, toward great simplicity, replacing the mystery and solemnity of Latin chant with rhythmic vernacular hymns in which all could participate. The Latin *spectacula,* as expressions of worship, were felt to be almost replusive. So too the worshipful approach of the Roman Mass, emphasizing the distance of the people from God, and the elevation of the sacrament, were commonly rejected in favor of a simple dramatization of unity among the members of the community.

Most problematic of all was the inability of the Church to devise methods of guidance for the peoples of the developing cultures of the North. The Roman model of authority, again majestic, in the figure of the imperial pope, surrounded by a nobility of cardinals and other officials of the court, symbolized, according to traditional cultural values of Rome, rule by the eternal law of God. But again this external form of the Church, however appropriate within one culture, was in fact offensive in terms of another culture. So the court of Rome was viewed by the Reformers as an abandonment of the Gospel for a complete plunge into worldliness and vice. Authority so clothed would completely fail to represent the law of God in such a different culture and would inspire little respect and less loyalty. Of course the Reformer's judgment on Roman culture was no more valid than Roman judgment on Germanic culture, but by their own cultural values it was difficult for the Reformers to see the

Church of Christ in a form of guidance that operated from an imperial remoteness and a thorough reliance on legal methods. They preferred the notion of community decisions, de-emphasizing hierarchical differentiation and urging personal responsibility.

The Church, having failed to incarnate itself in these northern cultures, failed to communicate its message through its theology, forms of worship, or ways of guiding Christian life. Certainly the incompatible commitments in dogma between the main Protestant churches and the Catholic Church are frequently exaggerated. The "revolt" insofar as it is described above, is really cultural variation. The modern emphasis on Scripture, liturgical emphasis on participation and community, and the developing role of the layman within the Catholic Church all show that there is no necessary separation of churches on account of differing cultural patterns. Had the Church been able to incarnate itself in the developing cultures of the North during the Renaissance, there is no reason to believe that the separation would have occurred or at least prove so permanent.

It is true, too, that for the most part the Church remained largely intact within the boundaries of the old Roman Empire, where it most fully embodied the culture and whose peoples were imbued with a culture very Latin in origin and growth. But for those of more northern countries, newly conscious of their cultural independence, a rigid adherence to Roman customs proved a greater price for unity than they were willing to pay. It is true that the Church of England retained much of Roman ceremony, but it quite definitely suffered the loss of popular support as a result. Even to this day, all the great popular religious movements, from the Puritans to the Methodists, have turned their back on the rich ceremony of the Established Church.

The Counter-Reformation saw great changes in the Church. The most obvious one was Her new position of diminished influence in Western culture. The Church no longer covered Europe, but was confined principally to southwestern Europe. Spain and Italy especially began to exert a molding influence on the cultural expression which became the stamp of the Church for centuries. In contrast, the outlying Catholic areas of Poland, Lithuania, and Ireland, though loyal to the Catholic Church, exerted little or no formative pressure on the development of theology and liturgy even within their own countries. The changes in the Church that occurred during and after the Counter-Reformation were Latin in inspiration, but these changes were intended for the whole Western church.

The Counter-Reformation was an age when the Church was sufficiently vital to bring about a notable change in Her forms of expression. But since this was purely a Latin affair, it resulted in the Church's becoming incarnate only in the Latin world. There, the contributions of the Church were powerful enough to inspire a significant cultural movement, a movement we recognize as Baroque.

Baroque art we are all familiar with, but Baroque is more than an artistic school; is it a distinct culture, expressing a whole Christian outlook for that age. We

had better take a close look at these Baroque forms
in the Church, since they have been a dominant influence in the Church from that time until the present.
Those familiar with the Church of recent years will recognize many of its lasting attitudes.

The Baroque culture attempted to picture the
universe as a manifestation of the glory and majesty
of God. In picturing God primarily as a king, rather
than as a creator in whom we have our being, or as a
Father who loves us as His sons, the Baroque choice inevitably stressed the more imperial attributes of God.
He must, for instance, be surrounded with majesty, and
creatures, who are His subjects, must strive to add
luster to His kingdom. He is, above all, the lawgiver
and ruler of the universe. All creation is subject to His
imperial rule, and all men must be brought to acknowledge the sovereignty of God and accept His law as the
guide of their actions.

But in fact the world is not totally obedient to the
law of God. There is evil in the world which prevents
this vision of God's triumphant reign from being perfectly fulfilled. Just as good is seen primarily as obedience to God's law, so evil is seen primarily as dis-
obedience. The presence of evil in the world means
that all is not obedient to God's law. The forces of
good, those obedient to God's law, must struggle
against the forces of evil, bringing all under obedience. There is no neutrality. All things human are
subject to the law of God. Whatever is not in obedience
is worthless or evil; it does not serve the glory of God.

This vision of the triumphant law of God can be
traced in Baroque examples of sacred art. Baroque

altars, for example, may appear at first to lack any single unifying plan because of the immense variety of elements which make them up. A variety of artistic forms, sculptures, and paintings, of colors, of subject matter, of angels, men, animals, and vegetation may all be clustered in or around the altar. However bewildering this may seem at first, it is an attempt to show the all-inclusiveness of God's kingdom, that all things add to the glory of God. Conflict is present, sometimes directly in depicting victory over Satan, or indirectly in the conflict of light and dark. This tumultuous variety reflects the struggle to incorporate all under the reign of God.

The *Spiritual Exercises* of St. Ignatius are another example of this mentality. St. Ignatius depicts the world as enrolled under two banners, that of Christ and that of Satan. The vitality of this arrangement is guaranteed by the necessary conflict between the two armies. Depending on whether or not one is obedient to the law of Christ, one is enrolled in one or the other army.

With their imaginations fed in such a way, it was natural for Roman churchmen to assume a rather combative stance and to see their duty as one of imposing the rule of God, the laws of the Church, on the peoples of the world. Instinctively, religion is viewed as the law of God versus the lawlessness of Satan.

The Baroque imagination did not limit its expression to a few architectural and literary works of art. The same view of the universe profoundly affected the whole Church, including nearly every aspect of Her teaching and practice.

The Church itself is a symbol of the divine Majesty. It stands mirroring on earth the glory of the court in heaven. The very structure of the Church is solemnly portrayed when the pope, carried on his *Sedia Gestatoria* and surrounded by the brilliant plumage of his cardinals, symbolizes through his formal magnificence the position of God as ruler of the universe. This helps to create an image of a pope gradually depersonalized into "Rome," who speaks divine revelation with exactitude, who is the detailed lawgiver, whose function it is to clear up divine ambiguities and weld the disparate elements of the Church into an orderly and unified reflection of the Empire of Heaven.

In Baroque terms, the single law of God is destined to rule the world. So the Gospel may be refined into a table of definitions which need not inspire one, need not even be understood, but which carry an awful burden of belief. Theological manuals of the post-Reformation period regularly devote much space, not only to explaining the definitions, but to the careful weighing up of the obligation which each carries with it: theological certitude, probable opinion, *de fide*, divine faith, divine and catholic faith, etc. With certain theological writers, by no means the most obscure, the degree of obligation to accept a theological point sometimes becomes more important than the message itself.

Baroque liturgy, too, revealed a tendency to become a formal rule, legislating through the rubrics each word, each gesture of the priest, who, separated from the congregation of spectators, prays to God in a language native to no man. By the distance in dress, language, and gesture from the natural human mode of expression, such a liturgy emphasized the dignity and majesty of "official" prayer and sacrifice.

It is probably in the use of authority in guiding the Christian people that most of us are conscious of imperial attitudes. Whether we consider moral theology, wherein the law of God, arrived at by a debating judiciary, is considered the ultimate argument; canon law and lesser diocesan regulations, which openly attempt both to inspire and to direct activity within the Church through impersonal legal means; or the famous Index of Forbidden Books, which seeks to influence even thinking by legal powers, the pattern is clear: leadership and guidance may be safely left to the legislative power of the Church. This, above all, is the human manifestation of the voice of God.

Today it is somewhat difficult to appreciate what a tremendously creative effort went into the Baroque church, one reason being that, since it was designed expressly for their culture, only Latins could fully appreciate the magnificence, or could even visualize magnificence as a suitable expression of Christ's Gospel. The other reason for our lurking distaste for a Baroque church is that Baroque culture died centuries ago, and we have had to go on pretending that we like it ever since. The Baroque church was the last fully developed incarnation of the Church in any culture, and as a result the Church has since been unable to seriously affect the development of culture anywhere.

Although it is unquestionable that the Church as a

whole has suffered from the lack of cultural openness, it is also true that nothing has suffered more acutely than the missionary activity of the Church. Early in the Church's history, previous to the division between East and West, there was throughout the Church, in each cultural area, freedom to evolve varying forms of human expression, so that we have surviving even now a wide array of liturgies and, sometimes outside the Church, varying theologies and systems of guiding the faithful that are far removed from the Latin church with which we are acquainted. The evangelization of the Balkans and Russia, to say nothing of areas within Italy itself, was accompanied by a free growth of local custom, so that the Church was closely identified with its local habitat.

The East-West schism helped to change all that, and the Reformation completed the change from a policy of encouraging cultural expression to one of conformity, even in details. The evangelization of Latin America, accidentally or not, occurred at a time when the indigenous cultures were in decline or collapsing, so that the willingness to accept Iberian cultural elements facilitated the acceptance of the Gospel. But since the Baroque age, precisely when the Church adopted a basic policy of conformity to the one cultural model of Rome, which only grudgingly allowed any variation, the Church has in fact failed to convert a single culture to Christianity. Although Catholics exist in every country, nowhere has a major cultural area become Christian during the last three hundred years, and this despite the fact that missioners have continued their attempts at evangelization. This failure of the Church is a startling and tragic fact which the missionary church must change.

The Colonial Church

To show the importance of cultural freedom in the Church and the result of its absence in missionary lands, it may help us to shift the point of view to that of the non-Westerner. What a non-Westerner may see in the Church is a Gothic building, staffed by foreigners who retain much of their own way of life, who explain the teachings of God in terms of European theology, who, in short, ask him to abandon his culture so that he may become a Christian. This, to the thoughtful observer, is not simply asking the hearer to accept the Gospel, but also to accept Western thought, Western art and symbolism, Western organization, and the Western way of doing things. It is, in short, religious imperialism, and no more acceptable than nonreligious imperialism.

In the eyes of non-Westerners, the Church seems too often to stand for religious colonization. When this happens the Church does not act as a leaven within the indigenous culture, attempting to enrich it. It does not show real interest in changing the culture, but instead chooses a policy of integral transplantation of the Roman Church. The missionary church is then seen as a foreign ship anchored in a domestic sea.

The preaching of the Gospel by such a church is sometimes fiercely resented. It is "proselytism" and appears to mean that the foreign church is recruiting more members away from the national culture for the "colony," and in this process the non-Westerner surrenders much of his cultural identity. An extreme example would be the Portuguese mission of Goa in India, geographically isolated, where converts even took a Western surname, seemingly to obliterate their identity. (In many areas converts are still expected to take a Western first name at baptism.) It is no surprise that India is one country where missioners are not welcome. We can expect that the growing autonomy of the non-Western world will only intensify this reaction against foreign colonization. The Church will suffer from this hostility to the degree that it has indulged in religious "colonization." The Church is all too frequently looked upon as a colonial church, a threat to cultural autonomy and independence.

We may complain that this judgment is unfair, since the Church has had a policy of respect for cultures. Nevertheless it must be admitted that the Church's actual practice has lagged considerably behind its theoretical position.

A church identified with a culturally aggressive West can never hope to persuade peoples of non-Western cultures to abandon their culture for the sake of the Gospel, especially since the Gospel is clearly distinguishable from the Western wrapping in which it comes. Christ may be acceptable everywhere, but Western cultural expression of Christianity is not. Ideally, the Church is not identifiable with any one culture, not even the Roman, but is the reflection of the Gospel in every culture.

The first step in the missionary effort is to determine what this Gospel is, what constitutes the essential message of the Church. The missionary church is the *presence* of God's teaching, grace, and guidance. By God's teaching we mean revelation, by grace is meant the means of grace, prayer and the sacraments, and by guidance we mean the organization and use of authority to guide the faithful in living a full Christian life. These essential elements of the Church are derived from Christ's command to "preach the gospel to every creature" (Mark 16:15), and "to make disciples of all nations, baptizing them in the name of the Father, and of the Son, and of the Holy Spirit, teaching them to observe all that I have commanded you" (Matt. 28:18-20).

This is the mission of the Church, and yet it can be realized only in human terms. The embodiment of the Church in different cultures means only that the Church fulfill Her mission by dispensing God's truth intelligibly, leading others to participate in a life of grace meaningfully, and shepherding them to eternal life effectively. God's teaching is "present" only when it is understood, and for this a local theology is necessary. To develop a local theology is to translate the Gospel into terms of a particular mentality and a particular culture. Truth, even God's truth, cannot be communicated without being communicated to someone and in terms which he understands. The Church cannot teach without teaching in a particular culture any more than man can speak without speaking in a particular language.

Similarly with the Church's forms of worship. The Church cannot symbolize or dramatize man's encounter with God in sacrifice, prayer, and the sacraments without following the symbolic language of a particular culture. A symbol that moves no one symbolizes nothing, is no symbol at all. Where the Church is using forms of worship, prayer, and sacraments which are symbolically meaningless to the people, liturgy is not "present" in that culture, and the Church is not fully visible there.

Clearly the same would be true of the Church's guidance of Her people. Leadership cannot be exercised without the cooperation of the followers. Patterns of behavior which establish leadership in one culture may thoroughly disqualify one in another culture. Where the Church attempts to direct and guide people through authority patterns which are not recognized and accepted as positions of leadership, through forms which cannot elicit enthusiasm, there is no guidance, and again the Church is not really "present." For the Church to be fully revealed in a culture, a local cultural form must be developed for each of these three elements. To fail in any one of them is to fail to make the Church "present" in that culture, and the Church will likely be seen as a colonial cancer, eating away at the spiritual vitals of a people, and as such resented.

Sovereignty and Collegiality

But even if we do come to an agreement as to what the Church's mission entails, by what means is the Church to bring about Her union with various cultures? This is the question which was debated in Vatican Council II and which we must face now. Since each culture is distinct, there can be no over-all plan of making the Church a visible expression of God's love other than the determination to be different in each case! This needed diversity of the Church's cultural expression received a great deal of discussion at the Council, especially in its close connection with the developing notion of collegiality.

Collegiality entails first of all the recognition that the bishops are the rulers of the Church, headed by the Bishop of Rome. The bishops are singly responsible for their own dioceses, but collectively, or in college, are responsible for the worldwide Church.

The notion of collegiality is not restricted to those with episcopal power. The clergy of a diocese are in union with the bishop, and for a fuller utilization of knowledge and talent, the priests should work together with the bishop in unity and charity to develop a local cultural expression of the Church. Finally, the whole people of God including the laymen have a place in this development, so that the parish priest must plan his attempts to give the Church a visible manifestation of Her nature in terms of the local culture in conjunction with the laity. It is not an individual or a group of individuals who can accomplish this task, but the whole local church actively working together.

The church of a cultural area is in a position to understand fully the cultural values with which it is dealing in its attempts to incarnate the Church. Nothing is less promising than the system of having foreign officials, who have no real contact with a specific culture, make decisions of what in that culture best expresses the nature of the Church. It is like translating a book into a language you do not understand. It would be sanguine to expect it to be understood, fatuous to hope for a best-seller.

Maximos IV, Patriarch of Antioch in Syria, delivered a remarkable address at Vatican Council II, from which I hope it is forgivable to quote extensively. Succinctly, the Patriarch states that "the problems of peoples must be settled by these people, and with them but never without them." [10] And though sometimes these sentiments have been interpreted largely in terms of national pride, Maximos IV is clearly aware of how much deeper the question is.

> In those countries with vast populations like China and India, countries with great and ancient civilizations which have nothing in common with the civilization of the Mediterranean, something more is needed, something which should be worked out with the help of Christianity itself. The same thing should be said about the African Churches, so rich in dynamic forces. There is a great work of radical adaptation which needs to be done so that these Churches may feel at home in language, mentality, customs, and usages. They must feel that Christianity is not something foreign for them, that it could be the soul of their soul. These peoples should enjoy a still greater inner autonomy than that of the Mediterranean countries, while keeping, above all this, the necessary link with the See of Peter. Only what is essential in the structure of the Church should be

[10] Maximos IV, "The Supreme Senate of the Catholic Church," in *Council Speeches of Vatican II*, p. 135.

required of them, as the First Council of Jerusalem decided long ago for the gentiles. After so much praiseworthy labor, dedication, expense, and sacrifice, can we say that Christianity has won the hearts of these people? Yet that is what must be done.[11]

This certainly is a comprehensive statement of the need for local autonomy in order to make possible the presence of the Church in every culture. In line with this reliance on local guides, Bishop Joachim Ammann of Germany suggested that Nuncios be done away with and that information about the Church come from the local bishops, for "these men would know the traditions, culture, *language*, and mentality of each region much more intimately and would be able to provide Rome . . . with much better information about conditions in their own territories." [12]

Cardinal Leger of Canada, in a plea for freedom and diversity, mentioned the specific areas where cultural accommodation is essential. "And perhaps we could admit, actually, that the Church, especially in recent centuries, has cultivated an exaggerated uniformity in doctrine, in worship, and in her general discipline."[13] The Cardinal also recognized that for the missioner, this freedom is considered absolutely essential. "Now many of the Fathers, especially from mission areas, have justly emphasized the importance for well-ordered missionary work of a strong statement saying that unity in the Church of Christ can

[11] *Ibid.*, pp. 136-37.
[12] Joachim Ammann, "Nunciatures," in *Council Speeches of Vatican II*, p. 140.
[13] Paul Emile Leger, "Freedom and Diversity," in *Council Speeches of Vatican II*, p. 222.

never stand in the way of legitimate liberty and diversity." [14]

This liberty is needed to accomplish the task of the Church's enculturation, which must be based in the first place on the recognition of the religious psychology of a people and the religious truths which it already possesses. The Bishops Conference of Burundi-Ruanda in Africa submitted an alternative text for the schema on the Church, which stated in part that "the authentic religious heritage of every religion, state, or person not only will not be destroyed in being offered to God, but will be raised to a more lofty and final dignity. It will contribute to the splendor of the Church, which should be progressively enriched with a greater variety of peoples." [15] To convert an area of the world does not entail the destruction of the culture any more than an individual conversion destroys the identity of the person.

What emerges from these proposals for missionary lands is the need for national synods of the bishops which have real authority to guide the development of a theology, a liturgy, and a discipline appropriate to the culture. Without this there is no Church which visibly expresses Her nature.

The Cosmopolitan Mission

The cultures in which the Church must be visibly expressed in order to evangelize them are not the au-

[14] *Ibid.*
[15] "The Church and Non-Christian Religions," introduction and suggested text, in *Council Speeches of Vatican II*, p. 274.

tonomous, isolated cultures of the past. Whereas a hundred years ago there was scarcely any exchange among Western cultures, African cultures, and Asiatic cultures, today it is clear that there scarcely remains a single area which is culturally independent of the rest of the world. This exchange among cultures begun by the West is not, as is sometimes said, a simple process of non-Western cultures being "Westernized," and does not destroy the cultural identity of any people. What is happening is that a new kind of culture is emerging all over the world, and since it is with this type of culture that the Church must deal now and in the forseeable future, it is worth examining somewhat carefully.

There are different types of culture and, in fact, some of the Church's mission areas are still among nomadic cultures. More of them are among largely agrarian cultures, and Japan's at least is a fully cosmopolitan culture. Nomadic cultures such as those of the Eskimos or some sections of New Guinea have not mastered the complex body of knowledge required to enable these peoples to remain in a fixed abode. Although they may grow crops, they lack knowledge of fertilizers, irrigation, crop rotation, and the leaving of fields fallow. They must often move on to fresh land. Such a society is a portable one and the people can possess and retain only what can be easily transported. Despite their fascination for anthropologists and the generous space allotted to them in missionary publications, nomadic cultures actually involve only a tiny portion of the non-Christian world.

Beyond the nomadic cultures are the agrarian cultures, which are considerably more numerous and more complex. With their knowledge of agriculture, these cultures make a settled life possible, and culminate in the development of urban leisure. With the greater organization and specialization needed to sustain settled agriculture, they possess law for property rights, engineering for surveying the land, irrigation, architecture for the storing of food, and many other mechanical skills. In addition, a system of writing to record all this, a system of education to transmit it, and a complex government to supervise this activity are called into being. This advance has been referred to as the "urban revolution" but this should not lead us to suppose that such a culture is of the same type as our own. For these cultures live by a peasantry which supports the whole, and although the centers of such cultures have enjoyed great cultural flourishing in art, literature, and religion, this is rather a superculture of the leisure classes, and bears no close connection with the laboring peasantry which supports it; this continues in the old established way almost completely unaffected by the successive waves of supercultural bloom and blight that sweep over the top. The basic culture is really agrarian and static, as in the old cultures of China, India, and Japan. Much of the art, literature, and religion that is dispensed to the peasants may serve as a justification of their predetermined way of life. For the very existence of the culture depends on the peasantry's continuing to till the fields. As long as a culture is basically agrarian, the binding of the peasant to the land is not arbitrary oppression, but the necessary terms for existence. The dreariness of serfdom and sumptuary laws is only the monotony of an agrarian culture.

In dealing with the static agrarian cultures of the recent past, the Church had only to acquire a mastery of it as one would a new language, through which to speak one's message in intelligible and agreeable terms and assume the posture of a religious leader, like Matteo Ricci in China or Robert de Nobili in India. For this type of apostolate the main preparation is in learning a new "language," the main task one of translation—translating the Gospel into terms of another culture. Once this is done there is no real new work remaining in such a static culture, but only a repetition of explaining, urging, and waiting.

A third type of culture is that which is dominant in leading countries and already initiated in nearly all others. This may be termed, somewhat clumsily, cosmopolitan, not because it is a monolith, but because there is intercommunication among these countries of the essential scientific information which is used as the motor force for social life. If the nomadic cultures are sustained by a few skills and the agrarian cultures are sustained by hierarchical supervision, cosmopolitan cultures are sustained by minds guided by scientific scholarship.

Such minds are employed in planning and guiding social life to a fulfillment of traditional cultural ideals which may vary from area to area. The difference between agrarian and cosmopolitan cultures can easily be seen. In the agrarian, permanent culture resides in the peasantry who support the over-seeing hierarchy, whereas in the cosmopolitan, the culture resides in those who possess the essential knowledge, in this case scientifically based thinking, so that the urban dwellers, as in the United States, through the government, actually support agriculture, whereas in agrarian cultures the situation is reversed. So too the cultural life of the agrarian workers is dependent on the city almost completely, changing from generation to generation in conformity with the urban life around it.

Science, in which we include any field susceptible of scholarly investigation and technical organization, continues to grow by intercultural sharing, and such elimination of isolation is itself a condition for becoming a cosmopolitan culture. Among these cultures there are no real secrets, for scholarship will not advance in isolation. Science and scholarship are not themselves the goal of a cosmopolitan culture, but the means by which previously desired goals of human life are pursued. Since it is itself indifferent to human values, science with its resulting technology can be indifferently utilized by any individual cosmopolitan culture for its peculiar ends as long as the necessary conditions for its own growth are maintained. Among these are a compulsory educational system leading to further investigation, a government and an economy that are open to its influence and that disseminate its results into the social fabric. A cosmopolitan culture is ultimately driven by its investigating minds in pursuit of the unfulfilled goals that are broadly indicated by its particular system of values.

A cosmopolitan culture is a culture in constant

flux because it has unrealized goals, which may be material prosperity, the achievement of minimum human dignity for its members, imperialism, world revolution, or any other goal, several of which may be found within any one culture. Cosmopolitan cultures tend to be pluralistic, since the investigation of specific goals and cultural values are themselves the subject of scholarly and philosophic debate. Scientifically informed debate on traditional values stimulates the decision for proximate and foreseeable goals and paves the way for planning and execution. This is the work of the intelligentsia, and however much we dislike the word, it is through them that a cosmopolitan culture survives.

The changing character of a cosmopolitan culture is assured by the continued advances made by scientific and scholarly investigation. This means that it is impossible to say anything of permanent accuracy about the structure of these cultures. One can detail the past, attempt to describe the fleeting present, or guess at the direction of the future, but unlike nomadic or agrarian cultures, cosmopolitan cultures cannot be firmly fixed in rigid cultural patterns. Our dependence on sociology, social psychology, motivational research, and public-opinion polls to describe ourselves year by year all attest to our consciousness of this fact. One result is that it is extremely difficult for anybody to keep up. It is a common experience to find that the unshakable convictions of one's youth in many areas have given way to hopeless confusion by middle age. A man's education, like everything else in a changing culture, suffers from rapid obsolescence.

Ten or twenty years are enough to ensure that an educated man who does not keep on learning soon ceases to be an educated man and becomes instead a hopeless anachronism. He has not changed, of course, but everything else has. No more than fifteen years ago, experts were assuring us that it was impossible for Japan ever to feed herself, though for several years now there has been a surplus of rice. Any thinking based on a fact that has died will necessarily die along with it.

It is a commonplace to hear that Japan is becoming or has become Westernized. Some reporters, more scrupulous, say that public life in Japan is Westernized while private life remains largely traditional. But what is meant by Western is not often made clear. That Japan has become a cosmopolitan culture and shares in the universal scholarship and technology is undoubtedly true, but this merely places Japan in a general type of culture and gives little indication which particular culture is meant, American, English, German, Italian, French, Russian, or what. In reality, it is none of these, but Japanese. For a particular culture can hardly be identified by the methodology which merely places it in the general type of culture. Cultural identification depends rather on the choice of values, the traditional values with continued alterations. This particularizes an individual culture of the cosmopolitan type and differentiates Japanese culture from American or French or any other. Japanese government, industry, and education, for example, are still of a distinctly Japanese pattern, rather than American or European.

Despite the free intellectual and technical exchange among different cultural areas, then, there is no loss of cultural identity, though there is certainly a loss of cultural stability. There are few static cultures left, and they will not be left for long, for the whole world is rapidly approaching a cosmopolitan type. This means that there is no perfect or eternal plan for giving the Church an adequate expression in India, for example, for India is changing year by year. The changing nature of cosmopolitan cultures, the more primitive of which are changing all the more rapidly, precludes any stable formula for making the Church "present" in a given culture. Vatican Council II could only call for the changes that are currently necessary. There is no way of foretelling what changes will be necessary in ten or twenty years. *Aggiornamento* is a continual necessity.

The necessity for the Church constantly to guarantee its effective presence in a culture as that culture grows, exists all over the world, in the traditionally Christian cultures of Europe as well as in non-Western cultures that have never been identified with the Church. In non-Western cultures, however, the problem is magnified, because the Western Church is so totally alien to these cultures. What is true of all cultures then, is pointedly revealed in a missionary country: that the Church can enlighten people's thinking, alter their lives, and guide their activities only insofar as its theology, liturgy, and discipline are adequate for these particular people, this culture.

We have said that the Baroque church today proves to be a lifeless thing, increasing, like crystals, only by monotonously imposing an exact pattern of itself everywhere it reaches, so that each church ideally is an exact duplicate of every other, like crystal to crystal. Though durable, such a church is brittle, and is not able to assimilate any new matter into itself. It is only by a free organic growth of the Church in a culture, selecting, like any living thing, the vivifying elements of Her environment and avoiding the poisonous, by adapting Herself to Her surroundings, that the Church can cover the earth. This requires, as we have mentioned, regional autonomy and continual effort to work out the necessary changes in each place.

Cultural Transformation in the Church

We can only talk about the "possibility" of a vital developing Church because the freedom to adapt the Church's outward form to a changing local culture does not guarantee that it will be successfully done. An intimate knowledge of cultural developments and a thoughtful judgment of which adaptations best express the Christian faith, which policy of the many possible best guides the faithful to a fuller Christian life, are both necessary. Freedom alone is not enough.

For example, the Church in the United States utilized the emerging public school system as a model for a Catholic school system. This bold adaptation would be most unlikely within the older, traditionally Baroque culture of Latin countries, where the non-Catholic or the secular is not regarded as offering fit models for anything Catholic. Although the U.S. bishops' decision for a Catholic school system is usually regarded as having been a brilliant move at the time, the changed culture of contemporary America has caused some to say that an altered policy is needed in today's changed circumstances. This criticism is causing a sort of crisis in the U.S. Catholic school system, and many resent any suggestion that our schools are not the eternal solution to our educational problems. The critics are sometimes considered "disloyal." But the willingness to re-examine how the Church may most effectively achieve its goals within a changing culture is the very thing that keeps the Church alive, the very thing that caused the Church in the U.S. to set up a separate school system in the first place.

There is no ultimate solution to the cultural expression of the Church. The ultimates in the Church are divine revelation, the sacramental means of sanctification, and the responsibility of the Church to direct Her people to a fuller Christian life. To put it even more simply, the unchanging part of the Church is the gift of God's teaching, grace, and guidance through human agency. But for the most effective form here and now, for these people at this moment in their cultural history, an enormous effort of cultural investigation, theological interpretation, and discussion must precede the formation and execution of any apt cultural expression of the Church.

Naturally this has an effect on the position of the active layman in the Church. The Church cannot well dispense with the services of cultural investigators, sociologists, and other observers who examine and interpret the changing contemporary scene. Nor, for that matter, can the Church change without a

similar change occurring in its members, as we see
in the effort for racial justice. Ultimately all members of the Church must assist both in gathering the
knowledge of cultural changes and in executing the
policies which develop from them.

If the changes forecast in Vatican Council II come
to pass, there will be changes everywhere, but those
in mission lands will appear almost revolutionary.
They will also be more difficult to bring about for
several reasons.

1. Non-Western cultures are not well known to
the Church. Especially where the Church is represented through foreign agents, an understanding of
the culture is not natural but is only arrived at
through serious study. In some places, perhaps most,
basic anthropological studies are far from adequate to
guide the Church's becoming indigenous in its manifestation. An adequate grasp of cultural change is
also required by agents of the Church if they are to
make the appropriate adaptations.

2. Non-Western cultures are changing faster. The
impact of the West, especially its knowledge and the
institutions dependent on it, education, industry, government bureaus, national health, to say nothing of
armies, is causing some dislocation in every culture
on earth, and the shape of the future has yet to be
molded for most of them. To lag seriously behind in
these cultural revolutions would mean that the Church
will have no voice in the future of these societies.
There is no time to be lost.

3. There is often no indigenous Christian tradition
to build upon. The practice of religious "colonization,"

at least on a small scale, has affected every mission land to some degree. And to the degree that there has been no development of indigenous cultural expression of the Church in theology, worship, and leadership, the task ahead is that much more complex.

Despite the difficulty and complexity of the task there is little doubt that the non-Western church must develop its own cultural expression if it is to become a part of the life of the people. Otherwise a Western theology may render the Gospel unintelligible, a Western liturgy may leave the people unmoved, and a Western authority may make them hostile.

Japan provides several advantages as a case for examination of the future of the missions. First of all, it is perhaps the first and certainly the most highly developed cosmopolitan culture that is both non-Western and non-Christian. This means that the Church is starting from scratch, with neither cultural nor religious affinities with the country. Japan has borne the brunt of the impact of Western science and technology (knowledge and its means of application), which have created a whole new series of institutions, compulsory education, industry, a modern government of economic planning and so forth, a pattern which is emerging all over the world.

The impact of science and technology which constitutes a cosmopolitan culture has also deprived the ancient sacral system of its vitality. Japan, having been through this experience, offers a testing ground for missiological policies, for determining whether our present practices are adequate or otherwise. Such an investigation should shed some light not only on missionary work in Japan but also, by analogy, on certain developments that can be expected by the Church in other non-Western, non-Christian cultures which are ten, twenty-five, or fifty years behind Japan in their development.

What seems likely to emerge from such an inquiry is that the Church, in order to achieve an adequate expression in a particular culture, must base its whole theology (translation of the Gospel into locally meaningful terms), liturgy, and discipline on cultural values already recognized. For this reason our study will begin with some of the major differences between the Japanese way of thinking and our own, especially the way of thinking in religious matters. We will then discuss the experience of the Church in Japan and attempt to show the probable direction of future developments.

Chapter II

JAPANESE RELIGIOUS PSYCHOLOGY

The title of this chapter may be misleading. Although it contains what I believe are some of the major elements in the pattern of conscious and unconscious attitudes of the Japanese toward religion, the choice is based on experience and does not enjoy independent verification by scientifically approved methods. At the outset it is important to be reminded that the factors here selected and explained are subject, therefore, to all the limitations of my experience and observation. But it is my conviction that these areas especially need to be carefully studied in order to delineate the mentality to which Christianity in Japan must appeal.

The Japanese's basic attitude toward himself and his outlook on society and the universe to which he is related form the underlying substance of his attitudes and feelings toward religion. These basic views appear to have been channeled into more specific aspirations by his religious background. Although I do not know to what degree a religious teaching—on nature, for example—is more the cause or more the effect of his similar attitude outside of religious contexts, for our purposes it does not matter. We are only trying to record the actual state of his attitudes.

The order in which we will discuss these feelings will be to consider the basic world view of Japanese culture insofar as it bears on religious attitudes and then to present briefly the current religious attitudes which seem to owe their development in the Japanese psyche to historical experience with the religions of Shinto, Buddhism, and more recently the new religions.

Psychological Unity

To elicit any serious commitment from the Japanese, one must take into consideration their psychic unity and consequent totality of response to any situation. In the West, we think of man's spirit as an amalgam of distinct powers and tendencies. With our love of analysis, we have dissected the human soul into innumerable fragments. We recognize an intellect and a will as distinct, we see reason usually in opposition to emotion; we have crude passions and delicate sensibilities. In addition, we have a psyche, an id, a superego, and miscellaneous archetypal patterns. This is an impressive array of interior forces, but they are all independent soldiers of fortune, which do not speak the same language and are mutually unintelligible, so there is no hope of a permanent peace. The spirit of Western man is like a broken-up jig-saw puzzle without a model. We cannot even imagine what the total picture looks like.

The Japanese, rather, consider their interior self to be a whole, a changing one, but a whole nonetheless. A Japanese will remain impervious to the most impeccable logic if he does not wish to face the conclusion. He sees the logic, of course, but it does not convince him of a truth unless he is willing to accept it on other grounds as well. As intellect and will are not independent, neither are reason and emotion opposed. If he has emotional objections against something, he does not see that it is reasonable; if he sees something as reasonable, his emotions accept it as well, for both reason and emotion must be satisfied for agreement. He reacts as a totality. Naturally there are Japanese who are relatively dispassionate in arriving at decisions and those who are relatively emotional, but it is only a question of proportion. In any case, there is a unified psychology of response. Until he feels this totality of impression, there will be no commitment. He tends to accept wholeheartedly or not at all.

This is of great importance in dealing with the Japanese, because we Westerners normally operate in the delusion that man is, or is supposed to be, a pure intellect. In an attempt to convince a Westerner, you may triumphantly squash his argument, and he may reluctantly admit that you are right; he will probably hate you for it and tell others that you are terribly proud and cocky. You may do the same to a Japanese, and he may cordially tell you that you have your view and he has his, and in his heart will sadly reflect that you do not understand, and will recall that he never cared for you particularly anyway. It is particularly futile to treat a Japanese as a disembodied spirit; for he is not, as we often are, ashamed of possessing feelings and giving them a voice in his convictions. He looks upon blind logic as a form of deceit, and wishes instead to see the whole picture before making up his mind. How will it affect his life? How will it alter his relationships? How trustworthy is the person who is telling you this? These are the questions he wants answered. As a result, the Japanese are usually slow and cautious in arriving at a conclusion, remaining noncommittal until they are satisfied on all points.

Because of the important differences in the Japanese psychology of response, it should be helpful to examine some of the important factors that help to shape that response.

The Family of Nature. The first of these is the intense feeling of the Japanese toward nature. The natural world is dearly treasured by the Japanese, and an appeal to nature will normally provide a pull toward assent. The esteem in which they hold nature and the affection they feel toward it are deeply rooted attitudes of the Japanese. Western man, though appreciative of natural beauty, particularly in its more awe-inspiring forms, tends to respect it only in its splendor and grandeur. For the rest, we tend to regard nature as a thing to be subjugated, wasteful until it is domesticated into an obedience and servitude to man's needs and desires. On the other hand a Japanese regards nature as his home, to which his sentiments are deeply attached. Furthermore, he feels that he himself belongs to the family, unlike us, who tend to regard nature as something separate from humanity, even though secretly we know we are as much a part of nature as anything else. The Japanese, longing to be a part of nature, have felt the necessity of being in harmony with it.

The Japanese love of flowers and their stunning flower arrangements are not simply due to a frank enjoyment of a beautiful object which has other equivalents. A flower cannot adequately be replaced by a man-made work of art with the same effect. The flower arrangement or the miniature garden somehow represent nature as a whole, and when a Japanese sees a flower, he sees not only the flower but the world of nature as well. It is, in part, a spiritual, nearly a religious experience and, as such, it is not surprising that flower arranging has long been associated with Zen Buddhism.

The depth of their affection for nature is apparent in that their experience of natural beauty is not only an enjoyable experience in itself, but constitutes a setting for motivation. Our enjoyment of beauty is largely a pleasurable end in itself, but to the Japanese it is a forceful means of attraction to something further, for it changes the disposition of his spirit. He feels at home, and consequently regards favorably any experience associated with it. Association with natural beauty seems to constitute an approval of nature for such an object. Temples and shrines in Japan, especially the older and more famous ones, are often surrounded by stately cryptomeria trees, which stand

like so many pillars supporting the sky, and many of
the smaller local ones are nestled among twisting,
sprawling pines, solemn, silent, and serene. It is fitting,
they feel, to enter a religious place through natural
beauty.

In addition to the attractiveness of natural set-
tings, the most compelling presentation of a point
of view is to show it as a part of nature. The new religions in Japan and especially Sōkagakkai, explain
their doctrines in terms of a natural process, which
to resist is to fight against nature. Failure to observe
their doctrine is not only the cause of all suffering,
but it is also futile. Nature is irresistible, and to oppose it is, to a Japanese, unthinkable.

The Japanese view of nature is sometimes vaguely
similar to the Japanese tendency to think in terms of
societies and groups of which they are members.
Nature is the all-embracing society of the universe. Although it is easy for them to see God as the head of it,
they find it difficult to imagine God as being outside
of nature. It is sometimes the tendency of Christian
theological explanations to stress the nothingness of
creation and the aloofness of God, making His interest
in this world arbitrary and difficult to visualize. It
would be more intelligible to the Japanese if we explained creation less as an architectural plan of God's
intellect, which is realized by an arbitrary act of God's
will, and more as a child or off-spring conceived by
God eternally and born in time, which He naturally
cares for as His own.

Thus all creation is the child of God, and man and
nature are brothers, a way of viewing the world to

which the Japanese are already committed. For surely there is a sense in which God and creation form one family, and God is the father of all. It would seem that to present creation more in this manner would be to present God's existence in terms that would make Him recognizable to the Japanese, and comprehensible to the present atheistic evolutionist, besides being closer to the terms in which Christ spoke.

It seems that the Japanese propensity to think of the spirit in terms of an unanalyzed totality is at least as good a basis for theological explanations of God as the Western habit of distinguishing in Him an intellect and a will, which does a certain subtle violence to the ultimate simplicity of God. Naturally, we must use the terms we have in speaking of God, but there does not seem to be any necessity for regarding God as an easily identifiable Westerner.

Japanese Argument. Westerners are generally agreed in looking upon truth as an absolute. A person who has otherwise despaired of all value in the universe is still likely to feel that truth has unqualified claims on the human person. If something is recognized as true, we feel we must accept it, regardless of consequences. In Japan, it is not so; truth is not regarded as absolute. Truth is recognized, but only as something useful or helpful. It never has absolute claims on the individual, because it is not greater than the individual. It is only a part of man and is his servant, So, one accepts as much truth as is good for him, as much as is beneficial. The perceiving mind alone can never force a Japanese to accept a truth he does not welcome. To be acceptable, a truth must find a place in his life. Truth is thus subjective, a part of the subject, and does not enjoy a separate existence in a sphere of absolute realities. Truth must be accommodated to fit into human life if it is to be acceptable. Lacking any clear perception of truth as eternal or obligatory, the Japanese must be presented with the truth not in absolutes, but in a human context. The way must be made smooth, humanized, for its acceptance.

Because of their disinclination to think of conviction as flowing exclusively from the mind, the Japanese tend to present even their arguments in terms of vicarious experiences that appeal to the whole person. In the West, we recognize at least two valid means of forming convictions, induction, or the wide sampling of similar instances to arrive at a general conclusion, which is the way of science, and deduction, or the logical inference of conclusions from what we already know, normally the means used in philosophy and theology. In contrast, the Japanese have their own special method of nonscientific induction, the presentation of one or more exemplifying cases, with no need of other substantiation. In presenting a talk or an essay, both the generalizing and the reasoning is regularly left to the reader or listener. One presents only the main idea and the experiences wherein one encounters the truth. This is the most common and most forceful type of presentation for the purpose of causing conviction and assent. This method of producing response does not attempt to compel assent, but by the concrete cases presented permits the listener or reader to encounter the truth through a vicarious experience, usually a personal one of the writer or speaker. It is an experience that is not so much intellectual as an experience of life, something analogous to the method of fiction. Again the basic psychic unity of the Japanese is honored in their method of convincing, sometimes confusing to a Westerner. A Westerner who understands Japanese may listen to a popular speaker tell what he is going to talk about, then apparently drop the subject for a series of graphically related adventures, which the audience obviously enjoy, but which, to the deepening puzzlement of the foreigner, bear only a faint relationship to each other and none at all to the "subject." Unperturbed, the speaker restates his personal convictions and stops, having made little apparent effort to unify his talk.

Yet his Japanese listeners come away entertained, expressing affection for the speaker, and convinced of his view. At first one has the curious sensation that he is the victim of a plot, since the reception of the talk seems as inexplicable and disproportionate as the machinelike laughter that follows even the most painful jokes of a television comedian. The Westerner's trouble is that he has been using only his mind, while everybody else has been living through the experiences related, which conspire to show him one truth. Nor is there any other way of presentation that is equally effective, for the average Japanese does not fully comprehend something until he feels that it has been experienced through his whole personality.

It seems that our logical presentation of Christian truths could be profitably replaced by the description of the experience of these truths in people's lives.

Social Harmony. The Japanese conceive of social life as communal action and a Japanese finds it difficult to commit himself to a society of which he has no experience. Given the commitment of loyalty and willing cooperation that is inseparable from membership in a society, the prospective convert to the Church or to any other society must carefully examine the implications of his membership, the obligation he is taking on, and the ramifications this will have in relation to his other social commitments. The first society to which he is committed is, of course, the family. Should a young inquirer's intention of joining the Church be opposed by the family, it is more than an argument between child and parent. It is a clash with family policy and a question of whether these two memberships are compatible or not. Westerners are likely to underestimate the importance of these "practical" difficulties, and unless directly apprised of them, will often not think of them at all. Yet in reality, the relationship between family membership and another membership will automatically be appraised by the inquirer and be an important factor in arriving at a decision. Before the considerable loosening of the highly unified family pattern after World War II, it was extremely difficult for a Japanese to abandon spiritually a traditionally Buddhist home, and this was one of the reasons for the snail-like pace of prewar conversions to Christianity.

Even today it is a major consideration with older people.

Nor is the family the only society to be considered. The company where a man works is another, and whether this permits him the time for Sunday worship and catechetical instruction is not the only problem involved. It is the demands on his loyalty as well as time that cause him to appraise the relationship of the two memberships. He may be asked by his employer to do something which the Church does not approve of. For example, an accountant who, under orders, must juggle the tax accounts, may feel not exactly that it is wrong but that he cannot be a Christian. He can neither demur to the implications of his company membership nor be disloyal to the Church membership. This may be a problem serious enough to keep a person from joining the Church. It is at least as much an emotional conflict as a problem of conscience.

The nation too is certainly a society about whose membership he must be circumspect. Consciousness of his loyalty to the nation may oblige him to defer membership in the Church, especially if he sees some government policy clash with the implications of his proposed Church membership. Any government policy, even though he may personally disagree with it, will have some hold on his loyalties. Privately he may believe what he wishes, often it is the correctness of the Christian view, but as a member of the nation he should go along with the policies.

Social harmony is of very great importance to the Japanese. Living in a turmoil of misunderstanding or unresolved difficulties is agonizing to him, and he will tolerate much, go to great lengths to avoid them. At least on the surface, Japanese politeness seems nearly infallible. There are even cases like the following. Two trucks crashed into each other. The drivers emerged unscathed and without a glance at each other, each looked at the damage to his own truck, shook his head, and muttered, "What a mess!" They probably felt much more upset than that, but until they had their feelings under control, they did not start talking to each other. Doubtless each had his opinion of the other's driving skill, but there was nothing to be gained by making it public. It would only cause everything to turn sour. After a bit, they spoke, presumably making arrangements for some kind of settlement, climbed into their trucks and drove off. Very likely they were still seething, but this was not visible. If a Japanese can help it, he never consciously discomforts another person, unless they are declared enemies. Any movement of his that disrupts this treasured harmony is a difficult one to make, so that a Japanese is unlikely to fight or argue for his convictions, even religious ones, if bad feelings with society will result. Social peace is regarded as a greater value than the defense of principles, and public manifestation of the dissenting individual conscience is considered bad form.

Greater attention should probably be paid to these problems whose solution is a prerequisite for a decision of membership in a society. It is difficult for a Japanese to commit himself piecemeal or halfheartedly; he moves best as a totality. Unless all these difficulties of relationships are ironed out, he will probably not act at all or even assent to Christianity unless he can assent to real membership.

Kimochi. In hearing English speakers converse in Japan about Japanese matters, from time to time you hear the word *kimochi*. This Japanese word is sprinkled liberally throughout the conversation of English speakers because there is no English equivalent, and because it is of such critical importance in things Japanese. The word itself is composed of two parts: *ki* meaning spirit and *mochi* meaning hold. Presumably the word could be transliterated as spirit-holding, but this does not tell us much. It is a word that expresses the total nonanalyzed state of one's interior spirit, and directly reflects the Japanese inclination to consider various facets of a situation as a unified whole. Normally it is a judgment of good and bad. If the reaction to a particular experience is favorable, the *kimochi* is good, if unfavorable, it is bad. Simple enough, until we recall that the total reaction to a situation is determined by a large number of elements, some of which we have just discussed. With this in mind, we find that it is difficult, often impossible, to analyze just how the *kimochi* is determined in a particular case. Everything must be favorable before one can confidently expect the verdict of a good *kimochi*.

In common with the little girl with the curl, when the *kimochi* is good, it is very very good, and when it is bad it is horrid. The *kimochi* is not only the total attitude toward any experience, covering the whole range of sensitive areas such as we have described separately, it is also final; from the *kimochi* there is no appeal. Reason or pleading, it all falls on deaf ears. Of course, the *kimochi* may change, but not until, by examination or accident, one hits on the sore spot and corrects it, if possible.

Anything unpleasant makes for a bad *kimochi*, and it is a very sensitive instrument. An inquirer at the Catholic Church, for example, may comprehend the teaching, be impressed by the ceremonies, drawn by the atmosphere, and willing to join in the activity, but if he has an unpleasant experience with someone at the church, the *kimochi* is bad, and it is all off. The Japanese have a delicate sensibility and are very careful not to offend and very solicitous to see that a person's desires are not ignored, aware that if the *kimochi* becomes bad, there is serious trouble. This is one of the reasons why a business organization in Japan takes such great pains in dealing with any aspect of its employees' lives. A good *kimochi* is necessary for smooth operations.

On the other hand, anything pleasant contributes to the formation of the all-important good *kimochi,* intellectual conviction being only one of many factors making up a good *kimochi* toward the Church. The relations of the individual with others and with the group he is dealing with are of central importance. Coolness, or even an absence of warmth on the part of those he deals with, tends to make the individual uncomfortable and hence leads to a bad *kimochi.* For an inquirer coming to the church, the friendliness shown him by individuals and a welcome reception by the group will often have more to do with determining his impression about Christianity than the most lucid explanation of its tenets. Yet both are necessary to be assured of a good *kimochi,* which itself is necessary for the continued attendance of the inquirer.

But the *kimochi* is not just a check list of major factors. It includes details we would consider infinitesimal. A Japanese bishop once told his audience of priests attending a catechetical conference that if the room one has set aside as a waiting room for inquirers is small and dingy, it will cause a bad *kimochi,* putting the inquirer in an unreceptive mood for the instruction to follow. But if a flower is added, it will make everything all right, for the waiting inquirer will look at the flower instead of the dirt. They will have a good *kimochi,* and your teaching will be received with a favorably disposed spirit instead of an unfavorable one. This calls for great attention to detail. To be assured of a good *kimochi* all factors must be favorable.

The psychological unity of the Japanese is such that, in areas of commitment, especially the acceptance of membership in a society such as the Church, it is essential to deal with them as totalities. In the presentation of Christianity, the position of nature in their outlook cannot be overlooked except at the price of incomprehensibility. They are not very willing to have nature relegated to a position where they find it unrecognizable. Likewise, the Japanese method of presenting ideas is ignored only at the cost of missing the most effective means of inducing firm convictions. Instead it would be most advantageous to use a method that is able to provoke instinctive assent. If, as in the Church, there is a deep interest in actually getting internal conviction, this is especially important.

It seems incumbent on anyone who is desirous of

accepting a new member into a society to make great
efforts to smooth away the difficulties it may involve
with all the other social groups of which the aspirant
is a member, from the family to the nation. It will require a complete assessment of the experiences the new
members encounter in the receiving society, lest there
be some unpleasant experiences, and justly dreaded
bad *kimochi* emerges from its lair.

Finally, it is a mistake to draw battle lines in the
Japanese soul, who unlike the Westerner, is unused to
viewing his spirit as a battleground. A Westerner may
enjoy making his most important commitments in the
heat of battle, when insane passions are raging without
cause, leaderless emotions are wandering to and fro, the
will in solemn disregard of the realities is pursuing its
own purposes, the intellect is issuing orders which
everyone ignores, while reason pleads vainly for a
truce and sentiment bemoans the unnecessary strife. A
Japanese will wait until the smoke of battle clears, when
all is quiet and everything is at peace, with only his sensibilities awake. It is out of this spirit that he is willing
to make a commitment to a new way of life, when he is
satisfied that he understands all of its implications.
When he chooses, he will choose wholeheartedly.

The Instinct for Community

Among the cultural traits of the Japanese whose
influence is both important and pervasive is their habit,
strange to us, of thinking of themselves primarily as a
part of a whole, a member of a group, rather than as

independent individuals. It is easy for them to consider the group's needs before their own.

One Western trait which is frequently a source of scandal to the Japanese is our tolerance, even encouragement, of a more or less selfish pursuit of private goals. The open approval of individualism in the Western world quite naturally results in a diminished sense of community responsibility, a price we are willing to pay. But to a Japanese the man who is socially irresponsible, who fails to think of the common good first, is considered as a human scarcely worthy of respect. Since to the average man individualism is instinctively offensive, many of the Japanese intelligentsia and university students have been unable to accept the whole of Western ideas on the pattern of human life without strong reservations.

For to the average Japanese, it is the society to which he belongs that rules his life and decides his actions. He considers this, quite without resentment or feelings of suppression, to be the natural pattern of social life. Whether we consider his nation, his political party, the company for which he works or the labor union to which he belongs, his religion, his school, or other associations, we will find that he looks upon these societies and his position in them in a similar way, reducible to the single analogue on which they are based —the extended family.

National feelings have always been strong among the Japanese, but this does not necessarily mean either that the Japanese are imperialistic or that they look down on other countries, even though this has sometimes been the case. Essentially, there is a heightened consciousness of their identity as a distinct people, of their membership in a group whose purposes they are willing to serve at the expense of their own. The Kamikaze, the suicidal pilots of World War II, testify to the depth and power of this feeling of the subordination of the individual to the nation. Whereas an American would tend to feel patriotism as a sentiment (love of country) and define his willingness to sacrifice himself for it by abstractions (fight for freedom, defense of democracy), the Japanese attitude is far simpler, though possibly deeper.

To a Japanese his nationality constitutes much of his identity, accepted naturally and uncritically like membership in a family, where loyalty can be presumed. Furthermore, like any natural society, the state is accepted as inevitably hierarchic, with the central government unshakably enthroned at the top. This is not to say that in Japan anarchy is impossible, but to most Japanese it is inconceivable. Of course the Japanese too criticize politicians, but the ruling politicians are not thought of as identical with the national government, which seems to enjoy a separate and privileged existence and whose decisions, even when contrary to one's personal opinion, are considered final. Only a dissenting political organization with its own national program is able to oppose the government.

The Japanese longing to live as a part of an organic group into whose purposes he is quite willing to submerge his individuality is seen also in the organization of many political parties. The consistent popularity of left-wing socialists among the intelligentsia, and the power of the student Communist organization (Zen-gakuren), testify to their predilection for communal thinking and feeling. Hence a political party such as the Socialist or Communist is not formed by the fortui-tous coincidence of individually desired policies, wherein each member may be pursuing his personal goals quite distinct from others, but it is something to which one belongs as to a family. A political party such as this is quite able to engage its members' deepest loyalties and most intense emotions, which may easily spill over into boundless fanaticism. Nor is this phe-nomenon peculiar to the left-wing groups. It was a stu-dent member of an extreme right-wing group who, in 1960, assassinated Asanuma Inajiro, the leader of the Socialist party, during a public lecture. It is a deep sat-isfaction to sacrifice oneself for the good of the society to which one belongs.

The same type of group consciousness that closely identifies the self with the organization to which one belongs is apparent even in commercial organizations. In Japan, to be employed by a company is much like accepting adoption into a family. Japanese indus-try is frequently characterized as being paternal, which is as accurate a description as is possible in one word, but it is inaccurate to suppose that the employee is reduced to the humiliating and distasteful position the word implies. For if the demands on the employee are great, often requiring him, even in prosperous com-panies, to work extra hours without extra pay and to give up his legally guaranteed annual vacation, even regularly, because he is needed, he still does not nec-essarily feel exploited, for he identifies himself with the company to an extent that our phrase "company man" scarcely suggests. Legal guarantees of workers' rights, such as minimum wages and annual vacations, though existing on the books, are curiously inoperative unless upheld by labor unions, based as they are on the concept of the individual's rights and hence unrelated to the accepted ideas of group or social membership. Japan is full of men who as students were radical left-wingers, but who, once they became members of a bank or industrial firm, have had their youthful indignation gently smothered by the comforting sense of belonging, which answers a much deeper need.

In becoming a member of the company, the employee naturally gives his loyalty and considers demands on that loyalty to be natural, at whatever cost to himself. Generally it is true that from small businesses to huge industries, the employees feel that self-sacrifice is both an inevitable and a just price to pay for a sense of solidarity with their group.

In contrast, factory workers of the lower echelons are normally assured of a fixed work week, but they escape lightly precisely because they are individually of less importance to the company, as they themselves are aware, and their sense of belonging is consequently less. But their relatively tenuous membership in the company family is likely to be compensated for by a full family membership in a union. The unskilled and semiskilled workers in large factories, who are not completely absorbed into "family" membership in the company, find joining a union irresistible, even though the strikes and demonstrations for which they must sacrifice their time and interests are often conducted less for their benefit than to further the political intentions of a remote politician, whose policies they do not necessarily understand or agree with. At least they belong.

Just because workers march in May Day parades or other demonstrations or deliver speeches at a union convention, it cannot at all be concluded that the opinions manifested represent the personal views of those involved. It is what the group has decided that is paramount, and it is considered every member's duty to go along with it, regardless of personal opinion. The individual's personal opinions, or at least the public voicing of them, is sacrificed to the whole.

Nor are religions in Japan entirely exempt from this type of social integrity. After World War II many new religions became popular in Japan, replacing the official Shinto religious sects which had been discredited by the defeat of the nation. The successfully organized new religions, principally Sōkagakkai, are highly centralized, fully constituted societies, which demand and get disciplined communal action from their members. Sōkagakkai especially, currently the most rapidly growing religion in Japan, requires a total commitment from its members. Like many other of the new religions, it sponsors its own political candidates, thus bringing even political action within its competence, and presenting to the world a picture of a complete way of life. It also closely supervises the lives of its members. Appointed members of the congregation decide what action should be taken in regard to a fellow member's personal problems. A religion exercising this degree of control is a type of religion unfamiliar to us. Unlike our notion of a religion of individual faith, such a religion is rather a religious society with an implied vow of obedience, and membership means something different. One cannot get this kind of religion by an interior act of faith; one joins the community, submits, and it is done. What to a Westerner may well be emotionally repulsive is to a Japanese emotionally satisfying. He is something because he belongs to something and is not just an unidentifiable portion of a faceless crowd.

Even in temporary or peripheral associations the depth and richness of membership is apparent. The Japanese educational system is not basically dependent on individual competition. Especially is this true on the compulsory educational levels, six years of primary and three years of middle school. They have an annual *undōkai,* or athletic day, on which, among other things, races are run. There is naturally a winner, but everybody receives some prize. All run, and all indeed receive the prize. Schools organize trips, and everybody naturally goes, since all are members of the group.

Nor is passing the course the concern in Japan that it is with us. In the first nine years of compulsory schooling a student passes inevitably, except for cases of prolonged illness. Even at the high-school and college levels the problem is not whether or not the members will graduate, for they will be graduated if they work at all. The difficult part is getting accepted as a member in the first place. Each year the entrance examinations for high school and college are so bitterly competitive that the season is called *shiken-jigoku,* or test-hell. It is at the pearly front gates that the issue is decided. For once in a school, to replace our fear of academic failure, the student is partly motivated by the loyalty he owes to the organization and the teachers.

Any organization, to the degree of its importance in the lives of its members, commands the same respect, loyalty, and sacrifice. This is even true of looser associations. If a merchant wishes to establish himself in a new city, for example a candy-store owner, he must first join the local organization of candy merchants. His competitors are probably less than enthusiastic over his arrival, but if, by due process of custom, he joins them, they are not permitted to drive him out of business, while he must agree to go along with the local policies with his active cooperation and support. An incident reported by an American oil company executive may illustrate the degree of interdependence they take for granted.

During the Suez Canal crisis, all the oil companies in Japan, of which there are many, not knowing how long the canal would be closed, over-chartered tankers in fear of a tanker shortage. The miscalculation was sufficient to drive the weaker companies out of existence. But as they were members of the Japanese oil companies' association, it was the duty of the more stable ones to help them out. Accordingly, the more powerful oil companies were assessed money by their organization to divide these losses among themselves, even though they too suffered similar losses. It was reported that when the Japanese head of an American-Japanese oil company explained to his American partner the action they would have to take, the American sighed and said, "I understand myself, but I don't know what the New York office is going to say." Even if it were known it would probably be unprintable.

But it is impossible to give more than a sketchy treatment of the wide range of such associations in Japan, for they permeate every area of social life. Perhaps the little said is yet enough to generalize about the nature of these groups and the basic pattern they follow. All of the associations we have discussed, the nation, political parties, commercial companies, religious organizations, and educational institutions, have some striking resemblances to the family. They are analogous in their hierarchical structure, their unity, and their ability to call forth personal involvement from their members.

The father of the family is responsible for the lives and welfare of the entire family, the mother follows his wishes but is normally in direct charge of the children and the management of the household, while the children are at the base with the least authority and responsibility, but owing obedience and loyalty. With similar clarity, these societies have well-defined gradations of responsibility. Each member of a group wishes to know exactly where he stands and what his responsibilities are, for knowing this he is almost literally at home.

Of a family it is fair to say that you either belong to it or you do not; you are either inside or outside. Japanese societies are composed of such insiders, who must be treated not only as functional parts of the organization, but also with consideration of their personal needs. It is important to remember that such "paternalistic" organizations are far from simple master-slave relationships. Although great loyalty is required from the members, great responsibilities devolve upon the leaders. Because it is unnecessary to trace the scope of the group's responsibility to each member in every type of group, we will speak only of a business group as a typical society.

Once a company hires a person, it also accepts him as a member of the company. There is, consequently, great reluctance to dismiss any employee, and management will endure recessions and even dishonesty on the part of its employees without firing them. There have been instances of embezzlers being kept on, for to dismiss an employee is analogous to throwing a member of the family out of the house. Only extreme provocation could cause such dismissal. Naturally, there are times when a business fails, but the employer must still do all in his power to get his former employees jobs. There were many instances immediately after World War II when former factory owners and army officers were sharing the little they had to care for those formerly under them, or for surviving members of their families. If you once belong to a group, this group will do all in its power to take care of you; it is a primary responsibility. The obligations resting on the leaders of any group are probably more onerous than those of the lowest member. Such are the burdens of paternity.

Such duties of the association toward its members are not restricted to times of crisis. The employees of any large and prosperous company can be expected to receive immense "fringe benefits." Company hospitals, housing, discount stores, and in some cases a company-operated high school for employees are provided, which in total value constitute something more than a "fringe," amounting at times to more than 50 percent of the employee's income. In addition, it is not uncommon for the job to pass from father to son, making membership almost hereditary. Nor do the responsibilities of the group toward the member end with providing sustenance. A typical wedding scene will find the best man to be the groom's employer and his wife the maid of honor. The employer feels responsible for seeing his employees married and may even have negotiated for the bride. There is no end to the benefits to be derived from belonging to a good company.

Even by these highly generalized examples, it can be seen how much is required of the group in looking after its individual members. The members of the group then, though they are quite willing to make heroic sacrifices for the group, have great expectations from any such association they may join. They are consequently quite critical of any failures on the part of the leaders. Should they fail notably, especially in fulfilling the purpose of the organization, its members are likely to repudiate the leaders, as happened to the military government when they lost the war. Leaders themselves tend to feel this responsibility for failure very keenly, even when such failure is not their fault. Retirement, disgrace, and even suicide are prices that have been paid for serious failure.

It should not be thought that because Japanese associations or groups are all on the model of an extended family they can therefore dispense with organization. On the contrary, such groups are very highly organized, for one of the important functions of any association is to keep the members informed at all times where they stand, what the current policies are, and what part they are expected to play in assisting in the execution of these policies. Every member of the group has a position on a graduated scale of a well-defined hierarchy. Arbitrary decisions which ignore these positions would be scarcely tolerable. Again, the member must be treated like an insider, not as a hired hand awaiting orders. To a remarkable degree, the member's external assent, at least, is normally solicited, and this necessitates an almost endless series of meetings, during which the moot point is discussed at great length. Members have quite a bit of freedom in expressing their opinions, even if the conclusion is foregone, as it often is. The desire to be informed and to know what is going on, even though it is not one's personal concern, is considered not more surprising in a large organization than in a family. For all these benefits, much planning and a highly efficient organization is necessary, only portions of it actually necessary to get the job done, the remainder to secure maximum cooperation and to keep every member happy.

Community Aspect of the Japanese Church. The Catholic Church is an organized religion. It is, of course, more than a mere society or group like others, since its vitality is dependent on the internal life of the individuals who compose it, and it is directed toward fruition in eternal life. The Church transcends the types of Japanese societies we have been discussing, yet it too has a visible presence, a form or organizational structure by which it operates in this world. Consequently, it has the appearance of one among other societies in Japan. In discussing the Church in Japan as a society, we do not describe the theological nature of the Church but only its presence in a temporary society, that of present-day Japanese culture. Our interest here is how the Church presents itself to the Japanese people, what loyalties it exacts, and what expectations it arouses.

Our predilection for individualism sometimes has unfortunate results in Japan. The Western missioner, especially, must often break old habits of thought. As a Westerner, he is inclined to think of a life of Christian faith almost entirely in terms of personal salvation, even to the extent of considering one's neighbor or the community as distinctly secondary, if at all. Charity itself is often reduced to a means of earning personal merit. This in spite of the Church's being the Mystical Body of Christ, whose members belong to one another.

To a Japanese non-Catholic who looks at the Church, the Church appears only as a society, since by definition he is ignorant of its eternal, theological nature. He cannot help thinking of this society in terms of the societies he already knows. His judgment about the Church will, in part, be based on how this society of the Church conforms to the pattern of ideal Japanese societies.

One of the first things he will notice is that the Catholic Church is only one of the Christian churches, and no explanation is adequate. Should a Catholic attempt to account for this division among Christians, he is more likely than not to hear the puzzled objection, "Isn't it the same Christ?" For the Japanese, whose ideal of a society presumes a very high degree of unity, requiring agreement from all parties and demanding cooperative action as postulates, the division of Christianity is a terrible scandal. A group of people with a common object who are unable to agree among themselves and spend their time in squabbles scarcely deserves the name of an organization. Any Christian church in Japan, because of its lack of unity with others, is already a partial failure as a society. As a result, the ecumenical movement within and among Christian churches is of great promise to the Japanese missions, and no doubt to others as well. Furthermore, any discoverable area of cooperative action with other Christian churches would seem to be a further means of closing this open wound, visible to all.

The Church in Japan, in so far as it is a society, evokes the same high degree of loyalty from its members as do other Japanese societies, which commit a person to cooperation and self-sacrifice in the area of external or social action. Of course the private, internal life of the member is his own, but what he does as a member in society is the concern of the whole group. It is the visible goals of the group that the member is committed to serve.

The willingness of Japanese Catholics to sacrifice the pursuit of individual intersts for the sake of working cooperatively for the Church surpasses anything we are used to in the West. In the United States one is fortunate to find 30 active members of the lay apostolate in a parish of 3,000 individuals, while in Japan a parish of 300 individuals may have as many lay apostles, a proportionate discrepancy of 10 to 1. This is partially accounted for by the higher ratio of priests to parishioners in Japan, but not completely so. The instinctive sense of responsibility toward working for the Church felt by the Japanese Catholics is certainly much of the reason, as can be seen in other ways.

Prominent Japanese Catholics, in accordance with their position, often show unusual zeal for the work of the Church.

A present judge on the World Court, Tanaka Kotaro, is distinguished for his writings not only in the field of law, but on Church matters, while his wife edits a Catholic periodical for children. Even while he was the busy Chief Justice of the Supreme Court in Japan, Dr. Tanaka found time for writing prefaces for many Catholic books published in Japan, and freely gave his time to meet with those who requested his assistance in doing Church work. Although Dr. Tanaka is outstanding, he in no sense stands alone. It is a general truth that a prominent Japanese Catholic will be notably cooperative in the work of the Church.

It is not unusual for widows whose children are grown up, and who have enough financial security to be relieved of working, to give all their time to Christian action, without remuneration. Men who presently hold responsible positions sometimes tell you that they plan to devote the rest of their lives to the spread of Catholicism when they retire. As a member of a society, their sense of obligation toward working for the purposes of the society is instinctive. The more power they possess to be effective in such work by way of talent, time, or position only increases their sense of responsibility.

But though Japanese are willing to cooperate in

joint action at great personal expense and even expect to do so, they also expect that their position and responsibilities will be clearly and precisely defined and orientated toward practical action. A sense of unity with and involvement in the purposes and activities of the society is considered essential for a full and fruitful membership.

This desire to share in the organized work of the society finds its fulfillment in serious and important activities. It is sometimes the practice in Japan, though less so than in the West, to put the women's group in charge of putting flowers on the altar, and the men in charge of organizing banquets, neither expecting nor demanding anything more from them. At this point it is well to recall that the purpose of the Church is not picking flowers or eating, but the salvation of souls. The running of the society of the Church is not expected to lead its members to trivial activity, but toward a personal involvment in the Church's mission. This point is worth emphasis. For if membership in a society means exactly defined position and precise responsibility in furthering the purpose of the society, the members will expect the proposal of higher goals, a more complex organization, more realistic planning of action, more serious discussion, and greater delegation of authority and responsibility than the traditional parochial pattern provides. In the West, with our emphasis on individual responsibility and personal action, we are not so completely dependent on group action. But among the Japanese, this type of group action is considered natural and if there is no such clearly defined basis of action, there is often no action at all. For the

Japanese find working in society in isolation extremely difficult if not impossible.

The Japanese Catholic will expect not only to be guided in his action of furthering the Kingdom of God in this world, but expects the Church to present a unified organization designed to achieve this end in which he has a clearly understood part to play. In addition, as a member of a society he has other expectations. These are the expectations of membership in a family-type society. He will expect consideration of himself as a person. A Japanese business or political party cannot be successful if it is content to treat its members purely as economic or political animals; a religious organization will be expected to treat its members as more than purely religious animals.

Most Japanese rectories receive a large number of calls from members who expect the priest to deal with their personal problems, however indirectly these are related to their specifically religious life. It is not altogether in fulfillment of their expectations for the priest to content himself with dispensing good advice. In the family-type relationship that is presumed to exist, the group, which is the Church in this case, is often expected to do something specific about the individual's problem. The member wants more than advice, he wants assistance. Being besieged by personal problems to a degree they were not used to has occasioned the remark among the earlier missioners in Japan that each Japanese Catholic requires his own priest. It would be more accurate to say that a member expects the group to care for him as a whole person and not just serve his religious needs. If there is no other provision in the group for the handling of such problems, the member will quite naturally take them to the priest. The Church both fulfills Her position as a society and relieves Her ministers by making maximum efforts to organize and deputize special groups to handle some of these problems. They often require delicate and prolonged treatment.

Arranging marriages is one of these areas where the Church's help is often solicited. In some parishes, often at the instigation of the laymen, attempts have been made to find suitable marriage partners for Catholics who are in the marriage market. Marriage arrangements generally are preceded by many meetings, involving go-betweens as well as the families of both sides. While setting up a Church marriage bureau among several neighboring parishes is certainly a helpful method, the drawn-out negotiations will still be required if it is to be fully successful.

Besides marriages, another important area is the member who is in some economic difficulty. Again to let each member shift for himself, as though it were purely his personal concern, would be considered heartless, not to say irresponsible. As a group the Church would be expected to do something for him—find employment or housing or supply sufficient goods to enable the individual to get back on his feet. Although considerable organization is necessary to deal adequately with these problems, yet it is expected that each of these people be dealt with personally. As members they belong, and expect to be dealt with as one of the family. A cold social-welfare service of the most mechanical type would certainly miss the mark altogether. It must be remembered that any society such as the Church is considered semiautonomous, and as such is expected to care for its members integrally. In a family-type society, each member must always be made to feel that he has not been mistaken in having chosen this society as his home.

Religious Feelings

The Japanese have their own way of thinking about a society, based on the structure of their own societies. They also have their own way of thinking about religion, based on the forms of their own religions. An examination of their religious psychology will, if it is successful, tell us what they look for in a religion, what they anticipate they must do to practice a religion, and what they expect a religion will do for them.

Exclusive of Christianity, there are three main categories of religions in Japan. The first is the native Shinto, the second Buddhism, adopted from China, and the third what is called the new religions, those which have been founded in this century from compounds of Shinto, Buddhism, and Christian elements. All of them have been influential in Japanese history, and all three have had important roles in forming the standards whereby the Japanese evaluate, consciously or not, any religion they encounter.

Shinto and Nationalism. The oldest among them, at least for the Japanese, is the native Shinto religion. It was the original religion of the Japanese people and, as such, is intimately bound up with myths of the origins of the country and the people. It is often felt as the vivifying and unifying spirit of the country and the people. It provides them with a sense of identity as a people and a sense of their uniqueness in relation to other peoples. Although it is a primitive type of religion and was largely replaced as a seriously spiritual religion by Buddhism over a thousand years ago, yet its nature as a native Japanese religion, fostering strong feelings of unity, made it consistently useful as a means of unifying the entire Japanese people.

A sense of national unity, the feeling of identity and unity of a people as a people, need not express itself as political nationalism—an antagonistic attitude toward other countries even when it does not break out in hostile expansion. Shinto provides a sense of national unity in several important ways. It has already been mentioned that cosmological myths, quite crude in nature, attempt to give a ground for or justification of national pride and a sense of unity. According to these myths, the Japanese islands and the Japanese people both are quasi-filial emanations of the gods. Even for the Japanese it is not necessary to accept these myths as literal truth, for they are equally efficacious when seen as a symbolic representation of the divinity and special position of the nation.

Being in some sense descendants of the gods, the Japanese quite naturally have a deep sense of reverence toward those from whom they received their inheritance, their ancestors. Their very high respect for their departed ancestors, something less than ancestor worship, results in religious customs of remembrance. In many homes a daily homage is paid at the family altar to the spirits of their forefathers which, as they explain, "comforts" the deceased. To what degree these spirits have a separate, substantial existence and in what sense they may be comforted is left undefined. What is perfectly clear is that the Japanese maintain by this means continuity with their forefathers, a very strong sense of unity as a people, and a sense of loyalty to tradition. Although this is a vague appearance of a sense of national unity, it nonetheless is a very deep and powerful means of sustaining it.

More dramatically and more tangibly, the emperor appears as the figure of national unity. He must make pilgrimages to the national Shinto shrine; he holds a position of at least titular head of some Shinto branches; even the wedding garment he wears is that of a Shinto priest and, of course, like many Japanese, he is married at a Shinto ceremony. The emperor and his centuries-old function of unifying the nation, symbolic since he has lost even the appearance of political power, is intimately tied to his position in the Shinto religion. And as the real rulers of Japan have always used the emperor as a breathing symbol of their authority, there has often been governmental encouragement of this national religion and it has sometimes been the official state religion. This was true of the militarist government in the late 30's and early 40's.

Immediately after World War II, the Son-of-god Emperor underwent a certain down-grading at the hands of the somewhat indignant victors. The Emperor, of course, never was the Son of God in the sense that he was the direct natural offspring of the creator of the world, but only divine in the vague, ill-defined manner which we have already suggested, symbolically the father of a people. The militarists who controlled Japanese politics in the late 30's until the end of World War II naturally did all they could to exalt the position of the Emperor and to encourage devotion to the official Shinto religion. If the motivation was less than sincere piety, it was certainly more than political cynicism. A strong feeling of national superiority, enthusiastically seen as a semiprovidential mission of the Japanese nation is probably a fairer picture. Given the propensity for national exaltation, Shinto always remains a convenient lever to tip a Japanese into chauvinism.

It is more difficult to assess Shinto as a religion. Much that is primitive and parochial in it suffices to exclude Shinto from the world's "higher" religions. Rather than a religion of faith, or a society of religion, Shinto is the ceremonial aspect of a feeling for nature and the nation, an emotionally charged symbolism of strong national consciousness. Thus it is a special form of national religion. But because of its long-standing popularity and its pervasive influence, it has been responsible for forming a specifically Japanese trait in their outlook on religion. Any religion including such mystical nationalism will be widely felt to be a fulfillment of a religious ideal. Sōkagakkai, as already mentioned, has extremely nationalistic tenets which in turn are based on the Nichiren sect, an extremely nationalistic sect of Buddhism founded in the thirteenth century.

Shinto itself has in fact been a great means of harnessing spiritual and emotional energies for nationalistic purposes. As such it is a horse that has drawn many political wagons.

Buddhism and Mysticism. If the original religion of the Japanese was the prelogical national myth and ceremony of Shinto, for well over a thousand years the Japanese have known a "higher" religion that seriously investigated the spiritual nature of man, defined his spiritual destiny, and showed ways of salvation. This, of course is Buddhism, or more accurately, many Buddhist sects.

Buddhism exists in many varieties, some of them widely divergent. No attempt will be made here to deal with all the sects which are present in Japan, for our interest is only in indicating what influence Japanese Buddhism has had in forming the opinions, ideals, expectations, and feelings about religion which are the patrimony of a modern Japanese mind. For though the present Japanese religious psychology is not exactly identical with the religious history of the nation, yet it is the conscious and unconscious residue of these historical experiences that does, in fact, constitute the present attitude toward religion.

A characteristic of Buddhism that is of immediate concern for our purposes is its extreme other-worldliness. The real world is elsewhere, in spiritual quietude, while the world in which we are presently immersed is a world of change and chaos, which is accorded only a quasi existence, and that reluctantly. For the world in which we live is an illusion, and should not be taken seriously. In the words of Bassho, the Japanese haiku poet, it is "a world of mist." However inadequate as an explanation of Japanese Buddhism, this characteristic nevertheless suggests an important corollary. Buddhism has no real interest in this world; a Buddhist's real interest is in withdrawing from it. Pre-eminently it is a religion of the spirit, not a religion of society. Quite naturally, Buddhism has no "members" in the sense of belonging to a family-type society. Such ties are antipathetic to its nature. Buddhism, it is true, must spread its own teaching, and the individual Buddhist must maintain an attitude of pity for all living and suffering things. Yet, in the end, there is little activity for the Buddhist to perform in this world; the only thing to be done is to withdraw and encourage others to do likewise. Although some organization is necessary to give any explanation of the way of salvation and to proffer opportunities for its practice, this activity is all turned inwards, toward feeding the spirit by starving oneself of the world.

Nor is knowledge of Buddhist teachings at all common among the Japanese. Virtually all Japanese are buried from a Buddhist temple, and many have visited the temples out of devotion, especially the one where their ancestors are buried, yet few have come away with any firm grasp of its teachings. Japanese Buddhism has never, until recently, been much of a teaching organization.

Although historically not deeply involved in teaching, Buddhism has brought the Japanese to a high degree of consciousness of the interior life of the spirit. By means of chants, images, temples, and especially by devotions and practices rather than by teaching, Buddhism has made the Japanese profoundly aware of their interior spirit as something separate and higher than the social life into which the body is plunged.

To exemplify the important ways in which Buddhism has formed the religious emotions of the Japanese, it may prove sufficient to restrict discussion to three representative sects of Buddhism in Japan, Shingon, Jōdō Shin, and Zen. Seeing how these sects have appealed to the Japanese should lead to an understanding of what he recognizes as a religious instinct, how he expects to enter the spiritual world, and what he is seeking from it. This last note of religious motivation is important, for whereas a temporal necessity is sufficient cause for belonging to a society, a motivating force within the individual is necessary to bring a person to this type of religion. It is already obvious that Buddhism has brought a deeper element to Japanese consciousness.

One important branch of Buddhism in Japan is the Shingon sect. Introduced comparatively early into Japan, Shingon places emphasis on incantations which are not literally intelligible, ritual gesture, and other symbolic forms of worship, all irreducible to strict intelligibility. The real world being illusory, these practices assist the devotee to arrive at a glimpse of a basic spiritual reality not perceivable through natural means. Partly as a result of this, the Japanese is unlikely to insist on clear intelligibility in religion. He is much more likely to feel that an attempt to understand religion perfectly is impossible and risks losing something of the necessarily nonrational essence of religion. An almost total absence of logical criticism as applied to religion and a preference for the obscurity of pure mysticism continues to characterize the Japanese outlook on religion to this day.

Several centuries later, but still about eight hundred years ago, the Jōdō Shin sect became quite popular in Japan. In many ways the most easily understood of Buddhist sects, this sect is popular by definition. Truly enlightened souls are able to achieve blessedness by themselves, but the average person is too immersed in the world to discipline himself sufficiently to merit this escape. For their sake, a Buddha, Amida or Kwannon, deferred his, or her, entrance into the Buddhist paradise until all men would be saved from this world. By means of Amida's merciful sacrifice, the seeker is assured of salvation. He has only to believe and call on Amida. The belief has the form of a simple, sincere desire and a prayer which is only an invocation of Amida's mercy by the phrase *"Namu Amida Butsu."* This is the famous *Nembutsu* or Buddhist prayer which every Japanese knows and which came to be regarded as efficacious in itself if pronounced even once.

Thus, in the end, Jōdō Shin has convinced the Japanese that a kind of quite effortless magic is the true nature of religion. The believer is almost carried to heaven by a momentary emotional surge. One result is that the Japanese is likely to have little difficulty in accepting an idea of faith. But he also tends to interpret it as a type of unreflective enthusiasm, almost wholly emotional in nature, under the influence of which he grasps salvation in an instant, and it is done. If the Shingon sect is partly responsible for having given the Japanese the idea that religion is pure mysticism, the Jōdō Shin sect is partly responsible for the current idea that religion is pure magic.

Of all forms of oriental religions that have achieved some notice in the West, Zen has certainly acquired the greatest notoriety and at least some following. In common with other forms of Buddhism, Zen has a lofty disinterest in worldly affairs, but unlike others, the Jōdō Shin sect especially, Zen is not directed upward to a paradise or forward to life after death; it is directed inward toward the cultivation of the individual's own spirit. What the Zen follower seeks is a mastery of the spirit which enables him to enjoy a spiritual self-sufficiency, independent of the turmoil and pain of a changing and illusory world.

By inward contemplation induced through special practices of concentration, Zen bestows on the adept a certain superiority to the uncertainties of the world in the form of a self-induced serenity and peace in which the subject's spirit becomes immersed. This deliberate cultivation of tranquillity is by means of an asceticism. But the asceticism is unusual in that it aims at a mastery over the world, rather than a simple denial of it. So asceticism is not practiced for its own sake but for attaining a posture of superiority toward the world. Although these disciplinary actions are performed for the sake of the spirit, and require great spiritual concentration and control of emotional energy, they are performed through the body. By poise of the body and solemnity of demeanor brought about by inward concentration of spirit, the Zen follower already accomplishes his mastery over material things in the world, for his body is part of it.

The training for mastery can be seen in the forms of discipline adopted by Zen. In Japan, the tea ceremony and a certain type of archery, both of which place the emphasis on form rather than on effectiveness, as well as the type of meditation known as Za-Zen, emphasize the close connection they feel between external demeanor and internal discipline. Each of these practices is really an art which is acquired through intense practice, though the intensity of the practice itself rather than the artistry displayed is the means by which the Zen follower attains the serenity and calm of self-possession. The religious spirit in Zen manifests itself as a state of utter calm, the quiescent spirit in a perfectly poised body which, as in the tea ceremony, is seemingly in repose even in action.

As a contributor to the religious psychology of the Japanese, Zen is particularly important as a source of the Japanese admiration for and desire of contemplative prayer. Of the expectations from religion, a state of inward serenity is often paramount. Even though a practice of meditation is considered religiously desirable, the practice may be valued higher than the matter meditated upon, as we have seen in Zen. There is no real object of prayer, such as the love of God for man; what is sought is the sensation of spiritual tranquillity, unruffled by the tumultuous world around one. Rather than prayer, it would perhaps be more accurate to say that Zen teaches the posture of prayer.

It is apparent how much these typical forms of Japanese Buddhism, so influential in forming the Japanese ideas on religion, concentrate on the interior life of the individual. The methods of approach to religious experience are quite intuitive and subjective, whether it is the Shingon believer witnessing a mystical ceremony, a Jōdō Shin believer uttering the *Nembutsu* with emotional intensity, or the Zen practitioner thinking the unthinkable in his rigid posture. None of this is easily communicable or susceptible of objective evaluation. Rather than emphasizing society, this type of religion largely ignores it, nearly dichotomizing man into the social man of daily life and the spiritual man of religion, with little if any defined relationship between them. Yet the high value such religious teaching places on the interior life of man, the separateness of the private and subjective life of the spirit, is assigned partly because in this man has a retreat from the omnicompetent and demanding societies which circumscribe so much of his life. To a Japanese, this is greatly appealing. From a religion, as distinct from a society, a Japanese is likely to expect to receive the spiritual benefits of peace, serenity, and a sense of the unshakable superiority of the human spirit over the world of change. This, probably more than anything else, is the most palpable religious yearning of the Japanese.

Elevated as it is in intention, this type of religious outlook, which depends on a withdrawal from the life of society into a private, subjective world, even though intense and disciplined, is subject in practice to debasement. There is sometimes a tendency among the Japanese to look upon religion as a crutch for the social cripple, which provides the believer with needed assistance for his journey through this world. The mystical penetration into a higher world provided by Shingon became little by little a mere refuge from the real one; the exultant grasp of salvation offered by Jōdō Shin turned into a terrified and desperate flight from the crushing brutalities of this world; while Zen practices, originally popular among leaders of society to fortify the spirit in order to ensure its mastery in dealing with society, slipped to the level of mental hygiene. In all these cases we see that the consistent propensity of the Japanese to choose what is useful for practical social life has made the preservation of an independently valuable spirituality difficult. It is very common among the Japanese to consider religions useful—for those who need it, those who require special fortification to endure the demands of social life. What in its origin was held to be food for strong and aspiring spirits, became in practice, medicine for the spiritual weakling. It is not unusual for shrines and temples to be utilized as spiritual clinics, and so devotions are widely believed to be a form of therapy. Especially by those who feel no need of such treatment, it is sometimes thought to be the only benefit religion has to offer.

New Religions and Social Mission. In the last few years, the phenomenon of the Japanese new religions, those that have been founded within the last hundred years, has attracted the attention of observers throughout the world by the great success they have enjoyed since World War II. Much has been written about Sōkagakkai, which is currently enjoying enormous increases in membership. We will discuss this more in detail later, but here it is important to realize that this particular religion is only the latest in a series of popular religious movements which are for the most part based on Shinto and Buddhism, though some have incorporated aspects of Christianity.

The success of the new religions is a dramatic manifestation of the vitality of religious aspirations in a modernized country. It is doubtful whether religion in Japan has ever generated as much enthusiasm among its followers as among the alleged 18 million members of the 171 new religions.

Since the life cycle of these religions tends to exhibit a period of rapid expansion followed by a longer period of relative stability, they may be open to the charge of being fads, but the continued existence of popular religions has led Harry Thomsen, in his book *The New Religions of Japan*[10] to look upon the phenomenal growth of the new religions as much more than a fad. He believes that they inaugurate a third major phase of Japanese religious history, the other two being the introduction of Buddhism in Japan in the sixth century and the foundation of the popular Buddhist sects in the thirteenth. There is little to contradict this. For the new religions have shown the ability to influence people's lives to a degree rarely matched by previous organized religions in Japan.

The new religions have contributed to the development of religious attitudes in the Japanese, and have also at times exploited them. One of the main trends exhibited by these religions, which is somewhat new in Japanese religious history, is in supplying religious motivation to the common people for involving themselves in the social and political life of the nation.

Since most of the membership of the new religions is in some six or eight of the sects, it should be possible to understand the central elements of the new religions by indicating what contributions have been made by these. For this purpose, it is convenient to group them

[10] Rutland, Vermont: Charles E. Tuttle Company, 1963.

in the three divisions used by those who have studied them.

The first group are the older ones, founded in the nineteenth century, Tenrikyo and Konkokyo. Both of these present God as the creator and parent-god of the universe. They are well organized and use modern methods of mass communications in spreading their tenets. Tenrikyo has a system of *hinokishin* or labor for the sect, which includes manual labor in building their headquarters. Konkokyo emphasizes social welfare.

The second group may be called the Omoto group, including Seicho no Ie and P L (Perfect Liberty) Kyodan. This group emphasizes the spiritual nature of the divine and the primacy of this divine spirit in man. Omoto itself has an international organization which discloses their interest in seeing the unification of the world as well as an emphasis on social work. Seicho no Ie has been politically active and endorses candidates for elective offices. P L Kyodan sees man as an artist and also promises world peace if all join them.

The third group is the Nichiren group, so called because of their basis in the nationalistic Nichiren sect of Buddhism founded in the thirteenth century. Besides its fundamental adherence to Nichiren Buddhism, Reiyukai shows great concern for social welfare, having a ladies' society and a youth society in order to help the sick and handicapped with gifts. Rissho Kosei Kai has group counseling, and proposes social-welfare service from the cradle to the grave. The remaining sect in this group is the better known Sōkagakkai, whose millions of militant members have caused consternation by their successful election of members to political office on their own ticket, and whose relative intolerance and nationalism have caused some to fear that they plan to make their religion the state religion.

This sketchy mention of some of the most important of the new religions is intended only to place the consideration of Sōkagakkai in some perspective. For the differences among the new religions are probably of less importance than their similarities. And these similarities, it seems to me, have had much to do with their success.

First is the often remarkable personalities of the founders. They may be poor, uneducated women and in fact often are, but regardless of their social qualifications for leadership, the founders appear to their followers as prophets who have been seized by the divine spirit and whose teachings are consequently of divine origin. In traditional Buddhist terminology, this original intuition approximates the flash of illumination known as *satori*; in the West, it may be compared to some unusually powerful "religious experience." Taniguchi Masaharu, the founder and leader of Seicho no Ie writes:

A light of truth flashed through my heart and dissolved my mental affliction. This manifest world, visible to the naked eye and felt with the five senses, is not God's creation. I was greatly mistaken in accusing and judging God. This world, as perceived with the five senses, is merely a production of our minds. God is love and mercy. The Real World, created by God's infinite wisdom, love, and life, is filled with eternal harmony. This Real World, this perfect and eternal world *always is*.[11]

Similarly, Nishida Tenko of the Ittoen religion received an enlightenment of man's position in God's universe. He should accept everything with joy, and abandon himself to God's guidance. Once he heard the voice of an infant crying out for its mother's milk subside immediately after receiving it. This experience gave Tenko-san an image of man's situation, which he analyzes thus:

> If man is born of God, God is responsible for his existence in this world. God should feed, clothe, and house his creature. Man should be glad to live and do whatever is good, even if on a modest scale, and simply wait for God to direct him to what he should do every day.[12]

It is but a short step from such inspirational moments, which are accepted as being of divine revelation, to the preaching of a kingdom of heaven on earth for those who are faithful to it. This is the second characteristic of the new religions: they are frequently messianic, promising a golden age of spiritual peace for their followers. In anticipation, one of the new religions, Sekai Kyuseikyo, has built two models of "paradise," with beautiful buildings and gardens at famous resorts. Connected with this is the importance of faith-healing, for the life of the blessed includes an end to sickness and suffering. This is also an important proof by visible

[11] Quoted in Thomsen, *op. cit.*, p. 154.
[12] *Ibid.*, p. 222.

facts of the rightness of one's faith. Immediate cures of all diseases are promised by most of these religions, often through some special ritual or prayer. The Japanese, with their traditional acceptance of karma, are susceptible to the belief that all human illness and misfortune must have a moral evil for a cause. This is quite difficult for a Westerner to accept as credible. Kitamura Sayo, the exuberant foundress of what is known as the "Dancing Religion," after explaining her teachings to an American university audience, was told, she reported, "Madam, if you are right, we are all mad here!"[13]

It would be a mistake, however, to think that these religions rely solely on the attractions of a visionary realm of bliss. Perhaps as important as anything else is their very efficient organization, which utilizes fully all the modern methods of propaganda and social psychology. The adherents have it drummed into them repeatedly that they must bring in converts, and the organizational structure of many of them is designed to facilitate this. The organization of Sōkagakkai, for example, is as follows: 15 families form a squad, 6 squads a company, 10 companies a local district, 30 districts a regional chapter, all under one central headquarters. Perhaps it is not surprising that a militaristic sect should resemble so closely a military organization. In addition, members are intensely trained in the methods of breaking down resistance in others and are guided by a handbook of arguments against other positions, Christianity included, to help them in their task.

Many of the religions use group counseling, pre-

[13] *Ibid.*, p. 206.

sided over by a leader who helps each participant with his problems. This certainly shows a keen appreciation of group dynamics. The method of group counseling permits the individual to receive personal attention and participation and binds him strongly to the group and the organization. Although this is certainly a departure from the traditional private subjectivity of religious feelings, it is founded on other Japanese practices. A troubled Japanese will normally seek a *Zadankai* or meeting with those from whom he has reason to expect help, and if he senses an atmosphere of acceptance and interest in the group, he is often quite unabashed in revealing himself, especially about his problem. That the new religions have embodied such a method in the heart of their organization only shows how scrupulously they may cater to the needs and expectations of the people.

No discussion of the various elements of the new religions quite does justice to the impact they have when they are actually seen in operation. To conclude our treatment, it might be helpful to concentrate on one of these, easily the most dynamic today, Sōkagakkai.

The structure of the Sōkagakkai religion seems to be a near perfect embodiment of a formula for a successful Japanese religion. On nearly every important point, it caters to the predispositions of the Japanese, both good and bad. First of all, and this is true of all the new religions, though pre-eminently true of this one, Sōkagakkai is a religious society highly organized to accomplish social goals. Although there is some inclusion of interior, traditionally religious psychology and emotion, the center of vitality is the social group,

with its demands for loyalty and sacrifice, cooperative action, and rather rigid control over external actions. This is a fulfillment of the ideals of a true society.
Secondly, it is a highly nationalistic religious movement. In this it gives concrete expression to the Japanese feeling of uniqueness of nationality, unifying the
ceremonial nationalism of Shinto with the political nationalism of the groups which manipulated Shinto, to
form one organization adequate to religious and political unity. Thirdly, it fulfills the religious expectation
of the many Japanese who look to religion for mystical
therapy or faith-healing. The magical reformation of
spirit which has traditionally been seen as a means to
function more effectively in the world, has been greatly
surpassed by Sōkagakkai. For not only do they claim
a spiritual cleansing that better equips one to achieve
success in the world, they offer a separate guarantee
that worldly success and financial betterment will automatically follow the acceptance of this new religion. It
would be difficult to surpass this in widely appreciated
and tangible benefits.

In addition, for the more scrupulous, and for the
modern Japanese who has acquired an independent respect for science, Sōkagakkai dispenses a pseudosci-
entific explanation of ultimate reality and the causes of
human ills, by which even the unknowable is presented
with comforting clarity. Like Communism, this religion
is aware that to present the most complex and obscure
realities as clear and obvious scientific facts is often ir-
resistibly seductive to the middling mind. "Why am I
suffering?" a man may ask. "Because you are exploited
by the capitalistic class," or "Because you are not in

harmony with the world spirit," comes the prompt re-joinder. Unable, or in his agony unwilling, to distin-guish between an explanation and a solution, he is ready to be told what to do. Explanations can be in-stantly supplied, but for a solution he must join a la-boriously slow-moving line that stretches far in the gen-eral direction of the future.

In the meantime there is much to be done: the re-organization of Japanese religious, social, and political life into an overpowering unity. Tailored for efficient social action, this religious society is notably active and effective in compelling others to join them, and notably indifferent to the acceptability of their tactics. One favorite tactic is "housewarming." A group of mem-bers, uninvited, enter the home of an unsuspecting non-member whom they hope to get to join. They begin to talk of their religion and attempt to interest the house-holder in it. They are not surprised at a polite expression of disinterest; they are not in the least deterred by it either. For now begins the process of breaking him or her down. First of all they stay. If they leave, as even-tually they must, they return again and again, for they know that the tolerant and hospitable Japanese finds it extremely difficult to refuse them entrance, unthink-able to ask them to leave. They become vigorous and vociferous in their arguments, while remaining deaf to all parrying remarks. With the maddening persistency of the true fanatic, they repeat their position, already clear, as though they were dealing with an eager but slow-witted child, instead of a thoroughly bored adult, whose nerves are beginning to fray. They do this with impunity, knowing that a deliberate insult will not be uttered by their victim and that because of the Japanese love of tranquillity, he becomes unsettled in the face of vehement opposition. Thus, the very virtues of the Japanese are used against them.

Finally, since the members are one homogeneous group, and the nonmember an individual, the householder is subtly placed at a disadvantage. It is the invading forces that constitute a monolithic society of insiders, and the householder (the term is becoming ironic) is reduced to the lonely nonconformist, and hence is an outsider. Like brainwashing, housewarming is designed to break down the opposition by depriving the victim of that which he longs for most. With Americans, this may be sleep, but with the Japanese, it is peace and tranquillity of spirit. He may have it as soon as he submits; his longing to be left in peace is often strong enough to cause surrender and accept membership. Once he has surrendered himself to this superior force, he will do what is expected of him, but he is used to doing so, and besides the same kind of tactic works as well with backsliders.

But though the means are hardly commendable, this is regarded as a justifiable way to enlist all Japanese in a unified effort of a national political group to create of Japan a religious-social-political unity, a worthy objective in many eyes. For with their long tradition and strong instinct for religious expression of political unity and national pride, many Japanese feel vaguely dissatisfied with even a good government if it provokes opposition and permits lax public morality, for a government that fails to unify evokes little enthusiasm. Sōkagakkai proposes to remake the country into a unified whole with an enforced moral code such as Japan possessed till the end of World War II. Such a proposal is attractive to many. The specifically religious elements in Sōkagakkai tend to be relegated to a secondary place. As the political activity of the group places more and more representatives in the Diet, Sōkagakkai emerges less as a religion than as a nationalist-political movement.

Religion and Atheism. From the foregoing account of Japanese patterns of religion it might be imagined that the Japanese are a religious people. Despite the number and variety of religions, the quality of many of them is such that they do not emphasize elements that we are accustomed to thinking of as inseparable from religion. Among these are an interior life of the spirit sustained by prayer, a demanding code of personal morality, and most importantly, faith in God. We have seen so little of faith in God in our account of Japanese religion because there is remarkably little there. What references to God or a divinity one is able to find in Japanese religions are likely to be vague, ill-defined allusions. As a result, the Japanese have never had a firm grasp on the existence and nature of God. Even devotees of religion, with only mythology to guide them, are unsure of whether there is a God or not and if so, what He might be like.

Against this fundamentally agnostic outlook on God, whose being is only hinted at in myth and symbol, the modern Japanese, particularly of the educated class, who have come to respect science, are likely to reject the notion of a Supreme Being altogether. Since even the shadowy existence of God was dependent on cosmological myths discredited by scientific thought, the young educated Japanese is likely to find atheism inescapable. Atheism is hardly surprising in a country that never had much of theism, indeed it is hardly an exaggeration to say that Japan is a nation of atheists, since atheism is compatible with some of their religions, Zen, for example. Clear rejection of the notion of a Supreme Being, however, has been reserved for more modern times.

As our earlier account of Shinto might have indicated, the world emanates from the gods, who are not distinct from nature. It is very difficult for a Japanese to grasp the idea of a creator distinct from the universe. Nor does modern Japanese education prepare the mind to grasp such an idea. With the origin of the world satisfactorily explained as a natural process by evolution, imaginatively only a subtle alteration of the old cosmological myths, the notion of a creator remains safely outside the range of the imaginable.

The problem of the existence of God forms a major obstacle to the acceptance of Christianity, probably the greatest. It is not unusual for a Japanese to attend catechetical instructions faithfully for some months, and then have him inform the teacher that his only problem is that he does not believe in the existence of God. This is sometimes the case even when the inquirer obviously wants to believe in God, and is weekly in attendance at Sunday Mass. Once the existence of God is accepted, the inquirer is unlikely to have intellectual difficulties with any of the rest of the teachings of the Church. Atheism, then, is a critical area of concern to which we shall have to return.

part two:

The Missionary Church in Japan

The [...] in preaching
the Gospel to the
Japan one must
consider the severe
limitations of the
part of [...] missionaries in
Japan.

Chapter III

PREACHING THE GOSPEL
TO THE JAPANESE

Through the foregoing account of the religious attitudes of the Japanese we are now able to understand better the object of the Church's efforts at evangelization, and to evaluate its activities. First of all, it will be necessary to place this activity in some perspective which reveals the severe limitations of the Church's mission in Japan.

Preaching the Gospel is not the simple activity it sounds. To preach you need hearers, and though much preaching is done, those who listen are quite naturally those who already believe. It is the old situation of preaching to the saved. The real problem is communicating the teachings of Christ and the Christian way of life to those who are ignorant of them. Being in the dark, they see no particular reason why they should investigate Christianity. Unlike the West, where even the non-Christian knows or thinks he knows a great deal about Christianity, Japan is a land which has never had a large Christian majority, and hence Christianity does not form a part of common knowledge. The Christian way of life is almost completely unknown. Before such a non-Christian can be expected to investigate Christianity, some understanding, some motivation must be already present. This much of a grasp of Christianity is a prerequisite for coming to listen seriously to the Word of God.

The average Japanese, with his nontheistic mentality and his instinctively low estimation of the importance of religion, is a particularly tough customer. The habit of considering religion to be composed of ceremony, magic, or therapy is hardly an advantageous beginning. Added to this is the frequent judgment, especially among the educated youth, that science is everything and religion is myth and hence not intellectually respectable. Confronted with a divided Christianity, each a tiny fragment in Japan, he is likely to be a disinterested and reluctant hearer of the Word. In fact, without a minor revolution in his thinking, he will be no hearer at all.

It is to such an audience that the Japanese Catholic must address himself. For it is the layman who, if anyone, will be able to make a change in his thinking sufficient to get him to consider the Church. It is possible to announce a new instruction class, advertise it to some degree throughout the area, and still have no one in attendance. Those who do come are mostly those who have had considerable contact with the Church through the speech and action of a Catholic. It is the Catholics who bring the non-Catholics within range of the Church's voice, and bringing someone with the adverse mentality we have just described is a delicate and prolonged operation. It is only within the limited range

of a Catholic's close associates that the dubious and suspicious non-Christian can get a glimpse of what the
Christian religion could mean in his life. At this point,
among these contacts, someone may show sufficient reaction to what he sees to indicate to the Catholic that
religion is more than he had thought. With this opportunity the Catholic may succeed in explaining something of his religion which will be understood. Assuming that this introduction to Christian matters is attractive, and that the non-Christian begins to think
seriously about the direction of his own life—and this
is assuming a lot—the non-Christian may be receptive
to an invitation to attend a church ceremony or church
lecture, and then for the first time does he have direct
contact with the Church; only then is he a possible listener.

The Church's message is in many ways far removed
from the consciousness of the average Japanese. Given
his unenviable religious background, religion as he
normally thinks of it is impossibly remote from his pre-
conceptions of life, his recognized problems, and his
conscious aspirations. Without an insight into the Christian life surpassing the experience of all but the interested friends of Christians, the Christian world appears as another land irrelevent to the life he daily lives.
It is no surprise that unshakable disinterest is his normal state. Disinterest can be expected to last as long
as no contacts are made with Christian life. The Catholic layman seems to be the normal agent of relevance,
able to display a Christian life which can form the non-
Christian's basis of appraisal.

Given these difficulties and the restricted area of

his personal contacts, the layman can be expected to devote much energy and much time to reach a single person at the depth necessary to provoke him to serious thought and churchward movement. The individual Christian is aware of this and yet commits himself to this task, which frequently exacts heroism. That his efforts have not been fruitless is apparent from the results of apostolic action since World War II. If we except the old churches of Kyushu because of their special circumstances, we find that the number of Catholics has grown from 50,000 to about 200,000 in the intervening 20 years, most of these newcomers having been brought in through contacts with Catholic laymen. But this does not give the entire picture, for we are interested here in trying to understand how widely the Gospel has been preached, not how many baptisms have followed the preaching.

Were we to attempt to count how many Japanese since World War II have actually heard the Gospel preached to them, we would have to settle for a rather wild estimate. Of any group of inquirers who listen long enough to form an adequate understanding of the Gospel, let us say attend half of a series of classes on the Church's teaching, it would be usual to find that at least one out of three or four receives baptism at the conclusion so there should be three or four times the number of those baptized who have heard the Gospel. But even this vague estimation of those non-Christians who have had the Gospel preached to them is misleading because of the large number of listeners in many classes who have been there before and dropped out for one reason or another. A new class does not nec-

essarily mean all new faces. Nonetheless if, at the outside, we multiply the approximately 150,000 postwar adult converts by four we still have the paltry figure of some 600,000.

In other ways, principally by observation of Catholics and conversations with them, or by reading, there
are larger numbers who know something of Christianity, but probably not much. The Protestant effort is
probably roughly similar to the Catholic one and would
probably have had similar results. But when all is said
and done, it is difficult to account for more than two
million non-Christian Japanese who have experienced
any presentation of the Gospel that could be considered adequate for understanding. In fact, the total figure is probably much less. Although this is an inconclusive estimation of the effects of Christian attempts
to preach the Gospel during the past twenty years, such
guesswork does call attention to the fact that preaching the Gospel to the Japanese is no easy task. We have
not succeeded in reaching with the Gospel some 98
percent of the people.

It still remains for the Church to preach the Gospel
to about 98 percent of the Japanese. With its growth
in fulfilling its primary mission, the Church in Japan is
still a young shoot. It is healthy and can be expected to
grow further, though not at a rate which permits one
to note a daily change. The life of the Church is long
and, in an environment which does not foster rapid
growth, impatience may dictate the feeling that it is not
growing at all, certainly an error. It is a tenacious
church, which the government with all its strength was
unable to uproot; it has endured storms and long

droughts and will doubtless do so again. But the growth continues, reaching, little by little, further and further, to cover the islands of Japan. It will take time, but this is only natural.

Occasionally, one reads casual references to "the rejection of Christianity by the Japanese." But who has done all this rejecting? Certainly not the 98 percent who have never heard the Gospel preached to them, and who have overheard only a few scattered remarks. It is like speaking of the "rejection" of the split-level house by the head-hunters of New Guinea. They have never seen one, and they have no idea what they are like. It would probably take deliberate and prolonged assaults on their sales resistance before many of them would make any sacrifice to have it for their own.

The missionary work of the Church in Japan has barely begun. No one will be able to speak at length or with assurance about the Japanese reception of the Gospel until the Gospel has been presented to many more millions than have heard it so far. Of all the limiting factors, the greatest is the sheer enormity of the task; Japan is the fifth largest country in the world, and to give an adequate explanation of Christianity to nearly 100 million people, the Church will have to speak for centuries.

Rome was not built in a day. Church historians habitually heap praise on the astounding growth of Christianity in the Roman Empire. Some account it a miracle, and even propose this growth as proof of the divinity of the Church. Yet in the first three hundred years of its existence, it is estimated that of the approximately 30 million persons in the empire, 10 percent or 3 million had become Christian, an average increase of about 10,000 a year. This is about the same as Japan. There is no reason to believe that the growth of the Church in Japan is significantly slower, nor that it has a less enviable destiny.

For those whose experience of Christianity is limited to that of the Western world, it is difficult to realize that the Christian Church is missionary by its very nature and that one who is a Christian is naturally also a missioner. The Church's responsibility is to witness to and preach Christianity to the whole world, to announce the good news of the Father's love, the Son's redemption of all men, and the gift of the Spirit to all who accept it. This responsibility is discharged through the actions of every Christian.

From the beginning of Christianity, inspired by Christ's last words as reported by St. Matthew, "Go and make disciples of all nations, baptizing them in the name of the Father, and of the Son, and of the Holy Spirit, teaching them to observe all that I have commanded you," the Church has seen this as Her mission. In the early centuries the expansion of the Church was a deliberate and continual effort throughout the extensive Roman Empire, and was continued after the Empire's fall until the peoples of Europe were nearly all accounted Christians.

What deserves emphasis in this growth of Christianity is that it was the work of the whole Church, with each believer accepting his missionary role. It was only when a country was "converted" that Christianity no longer included an exercise of missionary work. For in the absence of a non-Christian populace around them, the individuals in a local church could scarcely do anything directly to further promote the Church's mission of announcing the good news to those who had not heard it. The Church's mission in what was apparently a safely Christian continent became the province of specialists like St. Francis, who attempted to preach to the Mohammedans, or St. Thomas, who wrote the *Summa contra gentiles* to confute them, or the Franciscans, who in the thirteenth century traveled to the Mongol Empire to bring the Gospel. But bringing the Gospel to those remote or hostile peoples who had not received it bore little relation to Christian life as it was known and practiced by the average believer. Distance and especially the barriers of language and culture were effective obstacles to the average Christian's participation in the mission of the Church.

However, in Spain and Portugal, where the presence of Moslems was a reminder all through the Middle Ages of the Church's unfinished mission, the exploration and discovery of new lands and new routes in the fifteenth century revealed to men's eyes more than opportunities for trade and adventure, for beyond this they saw new lands to be conquered for Christ. A motive of sustained importance in this entire remarkable enterprise was the making of disciples of all nations, the East and West Indies, Central and South America, India and Japan. But when Iberian energies waned, Christians were no longer united to continue the effort. Were it not for the Reformation, it is likely that much of the world would have been Christianized during the intervening time and with the energies Protestants and

Catholics spent fighting each other and maintaining an uneasy and suspicious peace. As it was, the split of Christianity meant a serious loss of this consciousness of mission, and there has not been a missionary effort since that seriously involved the resources of the whole Church.

And yet, for a realization of the Church's missionary goal within any cultural area, the whole church within that area must be dedicated to the pursuit of its mission. Without the church itself being missionary in its every expression and action, there is no real mission work. The preaching of the Gospel to non-Christians is not a supererogatory activity of certain individuals, but the whole local church in action, speaking to the non-Christians in its midst by its very nature. Where there is a missionary church, it is where the whole church exists as a living Gospel being constantly preached to the surrounding nonbelievers. Being the activity of the whole church, everyone in it must share in this activity, bishops, priests, and laymen.

Ultimately then, it is impossible to separate the Church from Her message. The Church and Her message are one. The Church cannot very well preach one thing and be another, and still be convincing in its preaching. The non-Christian will be unmoved if he hears one thing and sees the opposite. The Church must strive to maintain a posture and a form expressing Her interest and concern for the non-Christians among whom She exists. And it is necessary to show a welcoming face toward outsiders which really manifests Christ calling His brothers, this in order to fulfill Her primary mission of making disciples of all peoples. In such areas, where the Church is "open" and all obstacles have been removed, there is where the Church is truly missionary. For in this case the light of the Gospel shines from the Church to a degree that it can be seen by outsiders. It is only where the Church is thus transparent that the Church can fully present Her message to the eyes of all men.

The Japanese Church as Missionary

If the history of the Church in the West has involved Her in situations where She tended to lose sight of Her apostolic mission, the same was true of a portion of the Church in Japan, though with far greater reason.

Christianity was first brought to Japan by St. Francis Xavier in 1549. Growth at first was only moderate, but on the southern island of Kyushu, many of the lords became Christian, at least some of them in the hope of attracting Portuguese trade, and compelled their retainers to accept the new religion. Many of these fell away. After some such early setbacks, the Church grew rather rapidly, still mostly in Kyushu, until the edict of persecution of 1614. By 1637, all priests were gone and all surviving Catholics driven underground, most of them to the islands off Kyushu and to villages near Nagasaki in Kyushu.

The persecution was of great severity and was continued sporadically, whenever the authorities discovered a group of Christians. These survived only where all or nearly all the villagers or inhabitants of an island were Catholic. That they survived at all is astounding. Hunted and having no priests, a number managed to pass the Christian faith from father to son until 1865, when a group approached, at his newly opened church in Nagasaki, a Father Petijean, the first priest who had been seen for some 230 years. But the traditional suspicion and hatred of Christianity was not ended. Persecution broke out again and some three thousand Catholics were exiled to remote parts of Japan. Only in 1873 did the persecution officially end. No exact figures are recorded of the number of crypto-Christians, since they declared themselves only gradually and some thousands are still aloof from the Church, but about twenty-five thousand approached the Catholic Church.

These Catholics were naturally almost the whole of the Church in Japan at the beginning, but they were in an unfortunate position to be the leaders in preaching the Gospel to their non-Christian neighbors. Long regarded with hatred and still regarded with suspicion, these Catholics were confined to a few Christian areas where they lived a ghettolike existence. For the most part extremely poor and poorly educated, they were long looked upon with disdain. Having always been isolated, they quite naturally maintained themselves aloof from the surrounding pagans, who so recently had been a threat to their lives. To this day there has been only moderate change. Although the number is three times what it was a century ago, the old Kyushu Catholics are still, many of them, isolated on remote islands or in villages where there are few non-Catholics, and the prevailing mentality is that "We are Catholics and they are not," and missionary work among the non-Catholics of the area is particularly difficult.

The Church in the other areas of Japan is very ho-

mogeneous and very different from the old Kyushu
Catholic Church, especially in its attitude toward the
Church's mission of spreading the teachings of the Gospel. For here the attitude of giving due importance to
the Church's apostolic mission developed without the
restrictions of any of the traditional fear of outsiders
that limited the Kyushu Catholics. And although Catholics in these other areas did encounter some of the traditional suspicion of the Japanese toward Christianity,
they did not encounter the hostility and disdain of the
southerner.

The growth of the Church was quite slow until the
end of World War II, for the attitude of the government remained partly suspicious and the Church's freedom waxed and waned at the whim of government
officials until it shrank to almost nothing under the
militaristic influence of the 30's and during the war.
So, in fact, although the attitude displayed by the Japanese church on spreading the Gospel has been lauda-
tory, it has only been free to show its missionary face
for twenty years.

During the postwar period the Church has made
consistent efforts to preach the Gospel. Its members,
bishops, clergy, and laymen, all have maintained a consciousness of the primacy among the Church's activities of making disciples. For this reason there exists in
Japan a church with a clear perspective of its mission
and one which promises to continue preaching the
Gospel among the many millions who know nothing of
Christian teaching. This, it seems, is a necessary disposition of the church if it is to continue to expand, and
it is much to the credit of the Japanese church that it

has retained a purity of insight into the nature of the Church and its mission. The church in Japan is not only one and Catholic but apostolic as well.

The introduction of the Church into any country is necessarily by foreign agents. We have already seen that it was St. Francis Xavier who introduced Christianity into Japan. He was followed by a generous contingent of Jesuits, who were later reinforced by Franciscans in the missionary work. The Jesuits opened a seminary for Japanese students, but this was cut short by the persecution before any great number of Japanese priests was forthcoming. After the opening of Japan in the nineteenth century, missionary groups from several countries sent priests, Brothers, and Sisters. After World War II, there was another wave of missionaries from many other countries, until at the present time nearly every European and American country has representatives among the foreign missionary personnel in Japan. In spite of the diversity of backgrounds, each group, motivated by the enormity of the task, maintains a unity of purpose in instructing their converts and forming their individual churches to be conscious of the Church's essential mission to reach all men with the message of Christ.

The contribution of foreign missioners in Japan is not at an end. The need will continue as long as there are large areas and large numbers of individuals who have never heard the Church's message. And this is likely to be for some time, for even now there is only one Catholic priest for every 65,000 Japanese, one parish church for every 175,000. With these figures alone to contemplate, it is clear that the Church is a long way from having given an adequate presentation of the Gospel to every Japanese.

But excepting the 1,200 foreign missionary priests working in Japan, the church in Japan is Japanese, and it is the missionary nature of this church which we must examine by noting the degree of apostolic awareness displayed by the Japanese hierarchy, clergy, and laity.

The apostolic awareness of the Japanese laity is very high, for most of them make serious efforts to invite members of their family, friends, and co-workers to join the Church and explain what they are able to of its teachings to their acquaintances. Nor does it end there. The Japanese layman is more than ordinarily aware of the apostolic dimensions of his job, whether in teaching, mass communications, or writing.

A critical factor in establishing the Church in a country is the institution of the local clergy and then the establishment of the indigenous hierarchy, for only then can the Church be said to be complete and independent in its structure. One of the most remarkable things about the Catholic Church in Japan is the very high proportion of vocations among men and even more remarkably among women. In a country where a large percentage of priests, Brothers, and Sisters are engaged in the work of spreading the Gospel, the desire to make disciples is probably a significant part of the motivation to the religious life on the part of many. The proportion of Japanese vocations is astoundingly high. Out of about 300,000 Catholics there are over 600 priests, which is a proportion of one priest to every 500 Catholics, one of the highest proportions in the world. Besides this there are 4,000 professed Japanese Sisters

and 250 Brothers, so that one of every 62 Japanese
Catholics is in the religious life. If we include seminar-
ians and nonprofessed religious, the proportion rises to
one in fifty. It is doubtful if the church in any other
country finds 2 percent of its members dedicating their
lives to the mission of the Church.

Numbers are not everything, but they are an index
to the fervor and responsibility of the members toward
the work of the Church. The more important factor for
our purpose is the attitude of the clergy toward preaching the Gospel. In some countries there is a percepti-
ble difference in outlook between clergy who are foreign missioners and those who are not. It is hardly surprising that the foreign missioner should be especially
conscious of the primacy of the Church's mission to
bring the Gospel to every creature, since he has left
his homeland for this very purpose. But, given the degree to which Catholics, clergy and laymen alike, have
tended to slight the mission of the Church in many
parts of the world, it is sometimes true, in mission
lands as in the West, that the local clergy are less conscious of the obligation to preach the Gospel to non-
Christians. As parishes get bigger, the responsibilities
involved in guiding Catholics to a fuller Christian life
can easily preoccupy the priest at the expense of his
efforts to reach new people, even in countries where
most people have never heard the Gospel. It is perhaps
natural that the danger is stronger for the indigenous
clergy.

In some mission lands it has been reported that this
is commonly the case. The local clergy, able to care for
the Catholics adequately, do not see that there is any-

thing else to do, even though 90 percent of those within the parish boundaries are non-Christians who have never had the teachings of Christ explained to them. But not in Japan. It is a hopeful sign that the Japanese clergy are no less devoted to the work of reaching non-Christians than are the foreign clergy, who came there explicitly for that purpose. With the continuance of this outlook, it is more than a hopeful sign; it is a guarantee that the Japanese church retains its apostolic nature, and as opportunity permits, will continue to spread the Gospel until it penetrates into every corner of the country.

If the Japanese clergy, already constituting nearly a third of the priests working in Japan, retain a high consciousness of the Church's mission to non-Christians and devote much of their time and energies to this goal, the same is true of the hierarchy. All of the dioceses in Japan are ruled by Japanese bishops who have continued to be extremely solicitous of the Church's apostolic needs. Although the high proportion of Japanese priests is sufficient, or nearly so, to care for the Catholics themselves, the bishops have continued to invite and welcome groups of foreign priests and religious to further the work of the Church. The Japanese bishops, while extending guidance and cooperation, have given foreign missionary groups great liberty in their pursuit of the mission work. Although an average diocese may contain missionary groups from four or five nations, the Japanese bishops, out of these diverse elements, have been able to weld a unified mission-oriented church. The cooperative efforts toward fulfilling the Church's apostolic mission are not limited to the individual dioceses, but extend to the country as a whole. The Japanese bishops have unified catechetical efforts by several means. They have provided a modern adult catechism for the entire nation which draws attention to the apostolic responsibilities of the layman, have established a national committee on the apostolate that studies and exchanges information throughout the country, and have founded a periodical for those working in the apostolate. They have done much more, of course, but the apostolic direction of these efforts has given Japanese Catholics a remarkable and admirable orientation toward making disciples of their fellow nationals.

Introduced into such a Church, the Japanese layman will quite naturally absorb much of its apostolic spirit, a factor of extreme importance. For non-Catholics are nearly always introduced to the Church through the agency of apostolic laymen. Whether drawn by the goodness of their lives, enlightened about a new way of life through their speech, or invited to the church by them, nearly all inquirers are the result of the apostolic labors of individual Catholic laymen. Without the laymen's consciousness of the Church's apostolic mission and their dedication to its goals, it is scarcely possible to establish the type of personal contact between the individual non-Christian and the Church that is so essential to the Japanese. It is a difficult thing to interest others in a religious way of life so different from what they know, and the Japanese layman must work with great patience and sacrifice to bring even one non-Christian to the Church. The numbers of Japanese who have succeeded in introducing a non-Christian to the

Church testify to the depth of concern they feel for this mission of the Church.

The Church in Japan is apparently solidly established as a church which has a full cognizance of its mission to bring the teachings of Christ and the experience of Christian life to every person in the country. To give an adequate description of the Church's way of answering this challenge, we must make some inquiry into the methods being used.

Chapter IV

AGENCIES OF THE APOSTOLATE

Besides parish centers, which will be discussed later, there are other means employed by the Church for the dissemination of Her message, means which cannot easily be limited to the boundaries of individual parishes. These represent the efforts made by the Church to reach the general public with the Gospel. One of these means is the lay apostolate as it is organized under national auspices, though it may have parochial branches, and professional groups which have apostolic activities directed toward the non-Christian world. Another category includes Catholic institutions whose activities are directed toward all those of a city or a region. These means include also mass-communications media as they are mobilized to reach a large area of the whole country. Finally, the apostolate among the intelligentsia must be included here.

In dealing with these three types of activity which in some ways transcend the local parishes, our interest will not be to regard them as services to Catholics or as organized charities, but only insofar as they are organs of announcing the Gospel message. Like the agencies of the apostolate within each parish, these agencies are addressed to particular groups of people more or less remote from Christianity.

Supraparochial Organizations

The first type are those which are local parish branches of a national organization. They are really part of the activities of the individual parishes, but their national character gives them a national unity and purpose and a complex organization that a parish in itself does not provide. One of such groups is the JOC, or Jocists, called Young Christian Workers in the United States. The Jocists are specifically designed for Christian penetration among the working class, and where there are local branches, their membership is likely to be composed principally of unmarried young men and women factory workers. The Gospel study outline and sometimes suggestions for activities are sent from the national headquarters, and the sense of unity is also maintained by annual regional and national conventions. The Jocists are true lay apostles, meeting each week and deciding on a weekly activity. Wherever a branch exists, its dedicated members make notable contributions.

The particular target area of their activity is the place where they work, the factory or office. The members are often effective in exercising leadership among their fellow workers in the problems of workers. They are also particularly effective in reaching non-Christians and interesting them in Christianity. Their interest and self-sacrifice on behalf of all the workers tends to give them an enviable position of leadership for attracting other workers to their Christian activities. In one parish, the eighteen members of the separate boys' and girls' Jocist groups counted among their number two officers of the factory dormitories, one head of a dormitory of 400 boys, and a factory delegate to a union convention. It is comparatively easy for such respected people to get a hearing from their worker friends on the Christian life. For besides their attempts to influence their milieu to reflect the Gospel truths, such apostles also introduce to the Church fellow workers whom they have especially influenced directly. These groups are an important means of bringing the Gospel to many workers within their place of work. The same two Jocist groups mentioned earlier were responsible for bringing many well disposed inquirers to the parish catechumenate. They have been in some parishes the most reliable source of new catechumens in the entire parish.

Somewhat similar to the Jocist organization is the Catholic Student Federation, also a national organization, which has prepared study aids, held national conventions and, like the Jocists, appointed deputies from national headquarters to visit each local chapter each year. This group also seems most effective when its activities are group activities, and as the Jocists have sometimes done, invites interested non-Christians to join the group without requiring previous membership in the Church. As with the Jocists, the sense of belonging to a national organization is a palpable influence in maintaining their vitality.

This kind of organized society, such as the Jocists

and the Student Federation, attempts to bring non-Christians within the sphere of the Church's influence. By working directly among non-Christians as a Christian group, they are able to involve interested non-Christians in a personal experience of a Christian social group. As such, they are an effective means of assisting interested non-Christians to make the last step to membership in the Church society.

Other groups, such as the Legion of Mary, may or may not operate in this fashion. Their purpose is to assist the priest in whatever work he asks them to undertake and so is not specifically designed to spread the Gospel among non-Christians. Where directly apostolic work is chosen for them, they too make direct personal contact with non-Christians in order to introduce them to the Church.

Still another kind of supraparochial organization is the professional groups, such as Catholic school teachers, nurses, and others. Again the primary purpose is not necessarily missionary with these groups. They may be exclusively concerned with guiding their Catholic members in living a full Christian life in their particular way of life. This type of activity falls outside our treatment. The modest size of most of the parishes in Japan usually means that in any one profession only a few, perhaps one or two, are involved, and hence on the parish level are unable to make any organized effort to spread the knowledge and appreciation of the Christian way of life.

The second type of apostolic means which are not entirely a part of the parochial organization are the educational, medical, and social institutions operated by the Church in Japan. Again it must be borne in mind that we are viewing them solely as agencies diffusing a knowledge of Christianity. These institutions are not directly aimed at spreading the Word of God, so that they cannot be considered to be direct attempts to bring non-Christians into the Church. They affect a broad band of people whose mentality is further from the Church than the interested individuals approached by members of lay-apostolate organizations and are effective in apostolic work principally through establishing contacts between individual non-Christians and some work of the Church. Unlike a parish, the area in which their effect is felt is usually a whole city or area rather than the section of a city where the building happens to be located.

The most important of these institutions which further the apostolate are schools. In Japan this includes colleges, high schools, middle schools, grade schools, and a large number of kindergartens which, unlike the other schools, are frequently attached to a parish church. There are in Japan 32 Catholic colleges, including junior colleges, over a hundred high schools, a similar number of middle schools, and some fifty grade schools. In addition are some special schools and about 450 kindergartens. Exclusive of the kindergartens there are over 100,000 students in these schools, of whom two-thirds are girls and about 10 percent Catholic. Given the large number of good public schools, some explanation of the popularity of Catholic schools among non-Christians seems to be necessary.

One of the reasons is that the scholastic standards of Catholic schools, especially middle and high schools, are high. Being private schools, the Church-operated schools usually call for stiffer entrance examinations to ensure the high intellectual qualifications of the student body. This naturally makes it desirable to get in, even for non-Christians. Another reason, especially applicable to the girls' schools, is that the Church has a reputation for giving strict moral training, which is highly regarded by the Japanese. Morality to the Japanese, it must be admitted, includes a heavy emphasis on deportment, and the Catholic girls' schools' good reputation for this interests many parents in sending their daughters to such a place. Being private schools and generally self-supporting means that the parents must expect to pay considerably more to get such training, but they are willing to do so. One result is that the students in Japanese schools, especially girls' schools, tend to come from rather high-income homes.

The wife of the present crown prince, who will one day be empress of Japan, is a graduate of the Tokyo girls' college run by the Religious of the Sacred Heart. This is not a freakish accident, for this school has long been a favorite college for daughters of wealthy and upper-class Japanese families. In many other areas, a similar situation prevails. The best Catholic girls' college or high school in the area is often considered by the middle and upper classes as one of the places to send their daughters. Among boys' schools this is not true to the same degree. Boys have more freedom in selecting their schools and employment opportunities rather than moral training is a greater motivation in selecting a school.

Schools provide an opportunity for contact with the

Church not only for the students who are taught Christian morality, but also for their families, who at private schools often have quite close relations with the school on the precollege level and especially so if it is a girls' school. Even though the parents do not become especially interested in the Church, they generally regard it favorably and are much less likely to place obstacles in the way of their children if they wish to become Christians.

In Japan, a school is a society as well as an educational institution. The student feels a close relationship with his school even after leaving it and will remain favorably disposed to the Church that sponsored it. In no schools do a large proportion of the students themselves become Catholics, but there is an annual group who do join. Since most of the students in Catholic schools are girls, many of the student converts are girls and since mixed marriages are the rule rather than the exception, these converts, especially if they were college students when they were baptized, frequently lead their families, including their husbands, into the Church. Still, the number of such converts is not large and the increase of knowledge of the Church and respect for Christianity on the part of the students and their families is in the long run quite possibly a more important contribution to the spreading of the Gospel. It is hard to estimate how much Catholic schools have contributed to the general high regard in which the Church is held by those who know it, but probably a great deal.

The large number of kindergartens, more than one for every two parishes, is accounted for by their popularity among the Japanese, the fact that they are normally privately operated, and that they are smaller and hence demand a comparatively small financial investment. Naturally, the mothers of the children must choose the school and bring the child there at least at the beginning. It is the mothers, if anyone, who stand to learn most about the Church through contact with these kindergartens. Many of these kindergartens are located at the parish center and provide an opportunity to see the Church. At the kindergarten it is not unusual to have special days when the mothers are invited to view the children's accomplishments. These days multiply the opportunities for informative contacts with the Church. There seems to be considerable variation, but if there are Sisters or others who pay special attention to the mothers, it sometimes leads to a serious interest in the Church on their part.

Of hospitals, there is less to say. There does not seem to be the same respect for medicine as there is for education among the Japanese. Most hospitals necessarily have a rather rapid turnover, and how much general hospitals are able to further the knowledge and appreciation of the Gospel through contacts with Christian charity is difficult to assess, though probably very little. Tuberculosis sanatariums abound in Japan, and some are under Catholic auspices. Here, because of the patients' length of stay it is possible for them to acquire a considerable understanding of Christianity, and it is not unusual for a patient spending a year or more there to become a member of the Church. In general, however, hospitals do not form an important part of the spreading of the Gospel in Japan. What the Church regards as charity, non-Christians are more likely to regard as business.

There are other social-service institutions such as old people's homes and orphanages. These institutions are no more productive of contacts leading to an appreciation of Christianity and are less effective as a means of the Church's growth. The old and the orphans are in such institutions precisely because they are not, for one reason or another, part of a family, so in most cases such contacts cannot lead to further contacts with families. Old people may often take an interest in religion, since this is traditional in Japan. With the Buddhist influence, religious practice seems to be a preparation for death, and has always been most popular among old people. Being in contact with Christianity, the old who are in a Catholic institution often adopt the Catholic religion, but this does not mean a great growth of the Church, for normally the faith will die with them. Orphans, except for those of high-school age, are of course too young to be admitted to membership in the Church. In summary, social-service institutions are not only founded for quite other purposes, but do not by their nature lead to the formation of many informative contacts between the Church and the non-Christian world.

Of those contacts which involve a large area of personal contacts with independent young people, the educational institutions in Japan easily have contributed the most to an understanding and appreciation of Christianity on the part of large numbers of non-Christians. Although there are some direct conversions through the schools, the deepest effect seems to be an awakening of interest and respect for the Church on the part of many who have come into contact with it through this means, parents as well as students. Although the range of influence of Catholic high schools or colleges is greater than that of an average parish, its effects are less deep. Reaching more people, schools move them less. But especially where close cooperation between parishes and schools is possible, schools may also directly assist in bringing many to cross the last line separating them from the Church.

Mass-Communications Media

These have the widest of coverages, but quite naturally have a much shallower effect. Their importance lies less in providing a complete understanding of Christianity than in being the necessary first step for the vast majority of those who know nothing of the Church and almost nothing of Christianity. Mass communications may provide the glimpse of Christianity which can arouse interest or admiration, thus moving a person one step closer to the Church. The biggest single problem faced by the use of mass media as a means of spreading the Gospel, however thinly, is the immensity of the competition. Mass media are everywhere employed, and the recent rapid growth of advertising has made the competition for man's attention all the more clamorous.

The Church's efforts in employing mass media as a means of increasing the consciousness of Christianity among the Japanese have been apparent from the beginning, notably in publications. The Japanese are among the greatest readers in the world. With a nearly total literacy, and gifted with great intellectual curiosity, the island Japanese rely heavily on the printed word for their knowledge of the world. Heavily stocked bookstores are everywhere and a town without one is a very small town indeed. These stores are favorite browsing places, especially for high-school and college students, who are insatiable readers. Besides books by Japanese authors, translations of European and American works are readily available and are quite popular. In 1955, 1,938 book publishers issued 137 million copies of books; according to surveys, half of the buyers were students.

There are only a few Catholic authors in Japan whose works have direct bearing on Christianity and are available at most bookstores. Most of the Catholic books published in Japan are published by one of the several Catholic book-publishing companies. Of their many publications, a high percentage are translations of books by European authors, many of them famous ones. The disadvantage is that Catholic publishers do not have the usual market outlets of the bigger Japanese publishing firms and, as a result, these books never reach the general public. The publication of Catholic books in Japan is primarily for the sake of Catholics. Even though there are many introductions to Christianity and to the Church among them, these books are rarely seen except at the local churches or at one of the few Catholic bookstores. Though advantageous to the Catholic, such an arrangement tends to limit severely the opportunities of the average Japanese to obtain a book which explains the Catholic Church. Any efforts which can be made to get simple, popular, introductory works on Christianity and the Church published by large publishing firms and so widely distributed would seem to be well worth it.

There is another factor which has limited the spread of Christianity through books. Most Catholic books in existence presume quite a thorough knowledge of Catholicism, and based on Western models, heavily accent a logical approach which is poorly adapted to the Japanese mentality. Even the official catechism, which is adequate for those entering the Church and for Catholics who wish to review the Church's teaching, is nearly unintelligible to the average unprepared Japanese. Similarly, the large number of commentaries and other books of exposition on Catholic doctrine are textbooks for study rather than introductory reading. The European and American books of apologetics are likewise designed principally for Catholics and presume an acquaintance with Christianity surpassing that of the average Japanese, even one who is intelligent and well educated. There are few easily understood books which could actually introduce the interested but uninformed Japanese to the meaning of Catholicism.

Until these two severe limitations are lifted, books will probably remain a weak tool in spreading the Gospel and in deepening the common understanding of the Church. The Bible remains the sole unqualified triumph in the use of publishing as an agency of the apostolate.

What is true of books applies also to magazines and

newspapers. Most of them are, even more than books, designed explicitly for Catholics and have little general interest. There is one Catholic magazine of high quality for general consumption, but this is a magazine for kindergarten use and the infant readers can hardly form any deep understanding of Christianity because of it. Attempts have been made to publish a national magazine of high quality and general appeal, but the magazine market is so crowded that newsstand distribution is almost out of the question.

The Catholic newspaper is even less promising as a means of reaching the non-Christian Japanese, for in Japan three or four huge newspapers with their local branches cover virtually the whole country, and there is just breathing space for local papers that emphasize local coverage. The steady customers that are necessary for periodicals in general and for the newspapers in particular certainly cannot be looked for among the disinterested mass of Japanese non-Christians.

Publications in general are a difficult field for a small group like the Japanese Catholic Church to compete in. Aside from single, popular books of introductions on Christianity and the Church, there seems to be little possible that has not already been tried. Even specialized periodicals have been attempted. The Jocists, for example, had a weekly newspaper designed for the working class in general, but it naturally tended to be a propaganda piece, lacking, as it did, the staff and organization to give competent coverage to all the news of the large and complex labor world in Japan. For distribution it was necessary to rely on pressing the

Jocist members into hawking newspapers, using valuable energy and time. There has been some success, but undeniably very modest.

Among the means used by the Church to reach the mass audience are the more modern channels of radio, television, and movies. Immediately after the war a Catholic radio station was set up in Tokyo. The venture floundered, probably for many reasons. First of all there is simply not enough daily material of a Christian nature to justify a whole radio station, and as commercial necessity asserts itself, any radio station tends to approximate any other. Secondly, within a few years after the end of World War II, efficiently run, popularly oriented radio stations were flourishing, many with nationwide hookups. Competition, both financial and artistic, was too heavy.

Although in different parts of the country some local radio programs were produced to reach the mass audience, the Catholic Church did not get firmly into nationwide radio programming until some years later. Preceding the Catholic effort was a half-hour program sponsored by the Lutherans and including a correspondence course, for which listeners could write in. The Catholic version consists of a daily five-minute program of a popular nature which emphasizes attractive morality by dramatic skits. It has proved to have a continued popularity and is now carried in every part of Japan, reportedly having a listening audience of 5 million. Connected with this program is a correspondence course for which listeners can write in, thus giving some check on its efficacy. Naturally such efforts are expensive. Besides the time to be bought, the expenses of production are not negligible and such a program is only sustained at considerable sacrifice.

Within more recent years, television has become widespread in Japan, most Japanese homes now containing a set. One of the first results of the popularity of television was the loss of the popularity of radio as the most effective means of mass communication. With television firmly established as the favorite means of mass communication, it offered a new challenge to the Church. If radio time is expensive and its programming demanding in time, talent, and expense, the demands are only multiplied in the television field.

Fortunately one Catholic agency, the Good Shepherd Movement, was able to put on short television shows of good quality that presented something of the Christian way of life on a weekly basis. Considering the tremendous outlay required, it was a triumph to be able to enter the field at all. Since television is the most powerful as well as the most popular means of mass communication, the victory is an important one. The competition presses for high-quality programming requiring a great financial burden, but television undoubtedly is a means of providing glimpses of Christianity to millions who have never been reached in any other way. More recently this program has been discontinued in favor of the production of movies which can be shown on television. Because of the rapid and unpredictable changes in this medium, there will probably be further alterations as conditions change, but the Church has shown that it intends to use this medium as much as possible.

Catholic movies have been used widely in private

showings in Japan, similar to our use of educational films. In the earlier postwar years, old films such as *Song of Bernadette* and *Monsieur Vincent* were frequently shown free of charge at parishes and at other convenient locations throughout the cities. Little by little the effectiveness of these films diminished as the Japanese film industry produced more quality films and as people, having more money, were able to see first-run films in comfortable theaters. The audience for such films became increasingly juvenile. With the growing number of television sets in homes, even children are unlikely to become enchanted with old movies in drafty halls. Such private showings are no longer effective.

Instead, the most effective outlet for films seems to be television. At least two full-length Catholic movies have been produced in Japan, but again, the difficulty faced by such production would be the problem of distribution.

The results of television and movie propaganda for Christianity are, by their very nature, extremely difficult to evaluate. Since it is a question of a more or less subtle alteration of outlook, nothing short of a highly refined investigation could yield any accurate appraisal of the results. The Church naturally operates in the area of mass communications without the guidance accorded to advertising agencies; there are no "sales" by which to measure the effects. Yet mass communications would seem to fulfill their purpose of informing if there is assurance that the efforts are patronized, the radio programs listened to and the television shows watched. This alone would suffice to prove that there is something there that non-Christians find attractive, and this is no small advance when complete indifference is the usual state.

All these agencies are directed to specific ends and to different circles of people. The circle of people who already know something of the Church and admire Her seem approachable through nationally organized activity groups or through local parochial branches. Though profiting from guidance and the material prepared by the national federations, these groups retain a locally rooted existence which permits the close personal contacts so essential to moving anyone to take the step across the threshold of the Church.

In the next circle of citywide or area penetration are the Catholic institutions, primarily the schools. Those directly affected are almost 90 percent non-Christians and presumably are better than indifferent toward the Church. Generally being excellent educational institutions, they attract quite a wide range of people, especially of the middle and upper classes, and permit contacts with students and their families which, though not specifically religious, still are based on a religiously or ethically oriented education. But because the school is an institution, the resulting contacts are less deeply felt than strictly personal contacts even though schools are looked upon as quasi societies, and the resultant loyalties are rather to the school itself than to the sponsoring Church. Nevertheless, the results certainly cannot be measured entirely in terms of on-the-spot conversions. By means of schools a comparatively large number of people take a significant step in the direction of the Church, as the nature of Christianity makes some penetration into their minds.

The mass-communications media are, by definition, addressed indiscriminately to all and can presume very little or nothing in the way of an understanding or appreciation of Christianity and the Church. While reaching everyone, they reach them on a rather superficial level. Impersonal and therefore unable to provide any direct contacts with the Church, such means are able to bring a regular follower to some grasp of Christianity, some vision of what the Church stands for.

In summing up, it can be fairly stated that the longer the reach, the weaker the grasp. All of the means mentioned are necessary, for very few people can be expected to embrace Christianity if they possess no more understanding of it than is current in Japan; few can be expected to enter the Church if they have not had contact with it in some form, and most will not choose it as a way of life who have not seen the Church operating in the form of a community.

The Apostolate of the Intelligentsia

In Japan, the intelligentsia are recognized as a distinct class, but the class is more inclusive than the term indicates in Western countries, embracing all educated persons whose subsequent occupation or interest relies on their education. Although the status of *intelligi* basically depends on one's college education, businessmen would not normally be included, but schoolteachers certainly would be, as teaching is regarded less as a job than as a social position of leadership. This is especially true for a college professor, one near the top.

The intelligentsia in Japan can be divided into four groups: scholars, writers, active leaders of movements, and university professors with their students. The Japanese scholar often differs from his Western colleague in motivation. The Westerner feels compelled to be motivated by a disinterested passion for truth, while the Japanese's personal interest in the subject needs no further justification. We often feel that truth is an absolute and that research is sustained by a disinterested love for it. The Japanese, with their disbelief in absolutes and their habitual consideration of the total personality, tend to feel somewhat differently. The work of the scholar is often considered to be a private enterprise of a subjective nature, much like the Buddhist notion of the interior life of a believer, which is unrelated to social life. This would apply less to the purely natural sciences, but even the present Emperor's known researches in marine biology are recognized as being a private pursuit, scarcely different from a hobby.

Although such research and scholarship is highly respected, it is not presumed to belong in the public domain, but remains within the private subjective world of the intellectual unless he writes or assumes social leadership based on his conclusions. In presenting ideas to society the process is one of personal involvement, and the idea remains relatively inextricable from the person who enunciates it.

Some priestly scholars have entered the field of scholarship as a form of the apostolate, notably some

Jesuits and some members of the Society of the Divine Word, which has a group of anthropologists in Japan, and have done scholarly work such as working with a group of Japanese scholars on a translation of James Joyce's *Ulysses*. Until the results of such labors become an active force through the writing of scholars they are likely to remain in the purely subjective domain.

Writers in Japan are important and influential intellectuals and their position in Japanese society is analogous to that of the French writer, who like Camus or Mauriac, though fiction writers, perhaps exert more influence through essays. In short, the Japanese writer, like the French, but unlike the American, is recognized as a philosopher, a guide to human life, and an arbiter of culture and politics. His presentation of his views, whether in newspapers, magazines, or book form, tends to be highly personal, if not subjective, for few ideas of cultural value are acceptable without the whole personality of the author behind it. The essay is a very important form in Japan, and Japanese writers consistently maintain their predilection for subjectivity and their suspicion of absolutes.

Shortly after the Hungarian uprising in 1956, the delegates of PEN, the international organization of writers, gathered in Japan for a convention. Since the Hungarian writers were influential in the uprising and particularly singled out for repressive measures when the uprising was crushed, the PEN delegates were prepared to issue a scathing statement condemning the ruthless crushing of freedom in Hungary. Much to the surprise of many and the open disgust of some Westerners, the Japanese writers refused to go along. Quite

apart from any Communist influences, they felt that
this incident did not touch their lives closely, and the
condemnation was couched in terms of "principles"
and "absolutes," which the Japanese do not readily
recognize, or feel deeply.

There is a high proportion of writers among Japanese Catholics, but of course their number and their
output is only a tiny fraction of the whole. Tanaka
Kotaro was one of the thirty-five great living Japanese
authors whose work was recently anthologized, published in one of a series of volumes issued by a large
publishing company. Rather surprisingly, one of the
influential writers in Japan was a French priest, Fr.
Candau, who died in 1956 and whose mastery of Japanese prose earned him a column in one of the four leading Japanese newspapers. Some of these essays were
later published in book form. But barring an occasional
genius, this is obviously a field for the Japanese, especially the layman, and if beginnings are an indication,
Christian writers will exert increasing influence in
Japan.

Active leadership in some movement provides a
broader avenue of influence for the Japanese intellectual. Political and cultural movements frequently depend on an intellectual for their foundation and for
their guidance. The intellectual has an opportunity to
guide the actions of groups by his thought, and a theorist
is visible behind most of the organized movements in
Japan. A notable example is socialism, but it is no less
true of the radical right. Women intellectuals, too,
have opportunities in Japan, where there are national organizations devoted to teaching housewives how to run

a better home and solve domestic problems. In the United States, such a function often shrinks to the size of advice-to-the-love-lorn, and columns of household hints in newspapers, whose authors easily escape the charge of being intellectuals, but in Japan even these areas are treated with some depth and taken seriously.

Active leadership provides opportunities for intellectual influence, but like-minded followers are necessary. The possibilities of an intellectual apostolate for Christianity is sharply limited by the general unpreparedness of the Japanese to participate in a Christian movement which they do not understand. Among non-Christians, only a movement which is indirectly Christian would provide an opening for the intellectual apostolate of the Church in the foreseeable future. However, a cultural movement that is started among Christians may spread to non-Christians as long as it makes only moderate demands for an understanding of Christianity. This seems one means of furthering the understanding of Christianity in Japan through intellectual means.

The field of the intellectual apostolate that contains the greatest number of people is that of the universities. The qualifications for work in universities and among college students are less specialized than that for scholarship, writing, or social leadership, and so open to more of the Church's agents. Moreover, college students because of their age and their interests are probably more receptive to new ways of life than any other class and they will lead the Japan of tomorrow. Due to these factors, the intellectual apostolate centered in

the university is one of the most promising in Japan and
deserves serious consideration.

Like most Japanese institutions that resemble those
of Western countries, universities embody important
traits that reflect Japanese cultural traditions. One is
the relation between professor and student. Traditionally, such a relationship is that of a master and his disciple. Like most relationships in Japan it is a highly
personal one. The master is responsible for the disciple
in a paternal way, not unlike the employer's responsibility for the employee. He would deal with the disciple
not simply as a student but as a complete human being.
Traditionally too, there is a very close bond between
the master and the disciple. If the disciple chooses a
teacher as his master, he accepts him as an advisor and
a guide, and will usually have great loyalty toward
him. A true disciple surrenders much of his independence in an atmosphere of trust. It is a spontaneous
act of trust on the part of the student that creates the
ideal relationship, and usually there is a confidence in
the master that is not easily shaken. The master is more
than one who imparts knowledge, he is accepted as
a leader as well.

Such relationships are easily perceived in the Japanese Church by anyone who has instructed inquirers
in the teachings of the Gospel. A foreign missionary
may begin with an impersonal exposition of the Gospel,
aiming only at intellectual conviction, but he quickly
finds that there is nothing impersonal about it at all.
While the teacher is explaining some point of doctrine
with a logic he imagines to be so devastating that it
cannot fail to convince, the listeners are placidly lis-

tening and wondering, "Is he someone I can trust? Will he understand me? Can I safely commit myself into his hands?" It is important not to ignore the personal relations between the teacher and the student, for much depends on this. When the listener accepts the teacher as a leader, all is serene; until he does, little of deep formation of mind will occur. In religious instruction especially, if the inquirer accepts the teacher as a leader, he will be likely to accept all he has to say; if he does not, there will be little or no conviction on any point. Again the Japanese psychological unity and totality of response asserts itself.

In colleges and universities, this traditional pattern will be considerably attenuated by the circumstances. A large number of students taking many subjects from several professors makes the teacher-student contacts relatively rapid and impersonal and their relationship tenuous. Many subjects are not very propitious for such master-disciple relations, because of their impersonal nature, but such subjects as philosophy, the social sciences, and literature normally involve judgment of human values and in these areas the teacher may greatly influence his students. He certainly will influence those who accept him as a master. Of course disciples are not made easily. Because of the degree of commitment normally involved in being a disciple, the student will be cautious in any selection of a master, carefully examining what the admired teacher has to say, slowly examining the person of the professor from every angle until he is satisfied that he is worthy and that he himself will benefit from his leadership. But once the choice is made, it will lead to a deep and lasting influence. If, in the eyes of a student, the professor is only dispensing information, this will not prove an occasion for a master-disciple relationship, but if there is discussion of an outlook on life, such a relation may occur. Anyone can give information, but only a master can form minds.

Unlike America, where the student's world-picture is pieced together largely from home influence, where ethical standards, cultural values, and even political opinions are often hereditary, in Japan the student's philosophy of life is critically examined in his university days, and he looks to the wisdom of professors for guidance rather than to the ties of home. In short, the Japanese college student is an intellectual at least while he is in school. Qualifying for a job may be sufficient motivation for college students in America, but seeking a philosophy of life is an additional desire of the college student in Japan.

As a result, university students are unsettled and searching for belief. They are also predisposed to accept a guide or leader in whom they can place confidence, by whose direction they will reach a decision on what system of values they will acknowledge. This makes the Japanese university student particularly susceptible to leadership. Nor is this search for guidance confined to theoretical areas. It is especially difficult to sell an idea to a Japanese if it is irrelevant to his life. In philosophy, as in religion, and in nearly everything else, a Japanese will normally think deeply about what he is commiting himself to before he accepts an idea. So it is only natural to act on what he accepts; this is part of his choice.

The demonstration and riots of the students in Tokyo a few years ago were very disturbing to foreign observers. These riots were under the leadership of the Zengakuren. The Zengakuren, the national student federation, is led by a small group of Communist students. The few top student leaders were actually "professional" students past normal college age, who registered each year in order to keep their student status, and had younger men serve as officers. What made this possible is the prevalence of Marxist thinking in the universities. Socialism is more common among professors, and it was significant that the Zengakuren was able to enlist wide student support only when it was demonstrating in conjunction with the Socialist party. Though this was by no means the only factor operating, a disciple would be expected to join an activity to which his master is known to be sympathetic. But such activity is only forthcoming when he has the student's idealism and freedom from clashing responsibilities. The more permanent and more common result is the formation of his philosophy of life.

The universities in Japan present a field for the apostolate which is extensive and at present the Church is no more able to give adequate coverage to this field than to the country in general. Universities are not evenly distributed throughout the country, but are concentrated in the larger cities, Tokyo, Osaka, and Kyoto. Tokyo especially is the principal city in this as in nearly everything else. The "Big Six" universities, which are in the first rank of Japanese universities, are all located in Tokyo, besides numerous universities and colleges of lower rank and smaller enrollment. Altogether, there are more than 300,000 college students in Tokyo.

Osaka is a distinct second, having some 80,000 college students and Kyoto is third with about 70,000. After this, the concentration of students in any one city diminishes rapidly, but no major city will be without one or more university or college. The college system is spread all over the country. Each prefecture, of which there are forty-six, has at least one public college in addition to private ones.

The receptivity of the college student, who is willing, even eager, to re-examine his philosophy of life, is such that the university and the college world is a necessary arena of the apostolate. There are already Catholic students and Catholic professors at these universities, though their proportion is very small. A university having 20,000 students would have, in accordance with the national proportion, only about 40 Catholics.

There is a Catholic Student Federation, already mentioned, which has local chapters at the larger universities, and these have a priest as their chaplain. But since in almost all cases the chaplain is not a full-time one, the contacts with the Catholic students are few and with non-Christians still fewer, sometimes nonexistent. In Tokyo, one chaplain may have to divide his time between two or three of the largest universities besides having a regular occupation. As a result, the average university student has little opportunity to come into contact with the Church or hear Her message. As a means of pursuing the intellectual apostolate, a part-time chaplaincy at a university, despite its importance, is inadequate to the opportunities. The students themselves are able to interest others, but they do not enjoy a position of leadership among their classmates, nor is there a Catholic center at the university where they may gather. The limited contacts with a priest and the absence of a community are severe limitations, for it means that the approach to Christianity is almost exclusively intellectual. The Church is never seen as a way of life or as a society. In such a cold, irreligious atmosphere, it is unlikely that many Japanese students would be deeply attracted to Christianity or to the Church.

Another means which has proved of great apostolic effectiveness is the student hostel conducted by the Church. Here the students live a life close to the Church, and have an opportunity to get to know Her more intimately. One such hostel in Kyoto has an average of 35 college students living with a priest. They follow the schedule set for them, which includes daily Mass. A weekly religion instruction is offered to them, and the priest is always there to help them with any problems they may have. Although nearly all the students are non-Christians on their arrival, during the course of their four years at the hostel over half of them eventually desire to become members of the Church. They have had an unusual opportunity to see the Church at close range and become familiar with it.

The effectiveness of such a hostel does not cease with conversions. During the first twelve years of its existence, this one hostel furnished eleven candidates for the priesthood. The intensity of the religious life they were leading gave them an opportunity to become acquainted with a religious life, much as it is lived in a seminary or monastery. When one considers the vocations that such a deliberate work with university students produces, the consequent multiplication of apostolic workers makes such a form of the apostolate more beneficial than almost any other.

Despite the gratifying results of this form of student apostolate, it still does not reach very far. It reaches a number of non-Christians on a very deep level, but has very little effect on the university itself. Most of the students will remain as unconscious of the existence of the Church, as ignorant of Her teachings as if there were no hostel. Some more far-reaching method that includes the mass of students is needed, permitting a broader avenue of approach to the Church for the majority of students. For this it seems necessary that the contacts of the Church's apostolate reach within the college or university itself.

Several priests have accepted positions as college instructors, who have the ideal position for influence on the students. One field that is especially open to foreigners is that of English, which is the second language in Japan, a reading knowledge of which is almost necessary if the student hopes to advance far in business or in any technical field. The advantage of this is that it places the priest in the position of becoming a possible master to some of the students, even though the subject itself does not suggest a serious involvement in a philosophy of life. The character and personality of the teacher is perhaps of greater importance than anything else.

A few years ago a collection of convert stories was published in Japan. In it were the stories of some twenty-nine converts who recounted the means by which they entered the Church. Among them were some two or three college professors who had attended the Tokyo Imperial University when Tanaka Kotaro was teaching law there. There was no mention of having studied under him, but the impact of his character, reputation, and kindly disposition were enough to awaken in those students a warm desire to follow his lead. One especially confessed that just knowing him, seeing him, was a powerful motivation for becoming a Catholic.

But generally, the apostolate within a university is more difficult for a layman, the principal problem being that no one knows he is a Christian. Regardless of his good character, it is not to be expected that the student will automatically connect this with his Christianity. Even if his religious commitment is known, the layman is likely to appear as a professor who just happens to be a Christian, and perhaps the professor himself will lack confidence in his ability to deal with religious matters when consulted. Such a position does seem to offer unusual opportunities to a priest. By his garb alone, he will be recognized as a religious person, one who is known to be living a religious life.

The position as a member of a faculty likewise places the apostolic priest in an enviable position *vis-à-vis* the other professors, his colleagues, for he appears to them also as a religious figure as well as a professional one. His apostolate should prove particularly effective among the professors if he himself has a serious interest in intellectual matters, if he proves informed and shows concern about cultural values and the direction of individual and social life.

Probably the single most important reason for the limited success of the university apostolate in Japan is that relatively few priests have been able to devote their lives to this type of work. Mostly the efforts have had to be spare-time attempts to accomplish a full-time job. It is to be hoped that at least for the larger universities, at least one full-time priest can devote all his time and energies to this critical apostolate in education. The students are the leaders of Japan's tomorrow. Among these will come the real intellectual apostles, the writers, and the leaders who will be able to guide Japan to a realization of the Gospel ideals in Japanese life.

Chapter V

THE PARISH AS AN APOSTOLIC CENTER

The Japanese Church is committed to making disciples of the non-Christians around it. To do so requires an organization, without which the Japanese find activity difficult but within which they are able to operate effectively. The basic organization of the Church is the parish, the local community of believers which constitutes a church possessing most of the essential ingredients of Christianity, the powers of preaching the Gospel, performing communal worship, dispensing sacraments, providing guidance for a full Christian life, and organizing a center from which missionary activity can radiate. The parish is where Catholics are born, nurtured in the faith, become mature in living it, and die. It is the form in which most people know the Church and as such is the natural agency of the apostolate. For not only are the children of Catholics "born" again into the Church at their local parish, but the parish is the gateway to the Church for converts as well.

With rare exceptions, it is at the parish church that

the inquirer hears the Gospel preached, where he comes in contact with the Christian society, and where he becomes a Christian himself. The parish is the vital cell from which grows the apostolate, the nucleus around which the layman's efforts to interest others is organized. To see in perspective how the parish works as a basis for the Church's mission to Japanese non-Christians, it is necessary to know where these parishes are located and what means they normally employ.

The great advantage of the parish as an agent of contact with the non-Christian world is its location, its visible presence among the people, within their neighborhood, beside their homes. Its effectiveness as a means for the Church to reach people who are strangers to it is based on this fact of accessibility to the people. In Japan it is not hard to find the people.

Tokyo is now the largest city in the world, having a population of over 10 million people, or more than 10 percent of the Japanese. Tokyo and the other five major cities, Osaka, Nagoya, Yokohama, Kyoto, and Kobe are all located on the same thin 350-mile strip on Japan's east coast. These six cities alone contain 18.5 million, and their concentration rather dramatically reveals the degree of urbanization which Japan enjoys—or suffers. These huge cities, all over a million in population, have always been large, but the great shift in favor of urban living has occurred quite recently. Whereas immediately after World War II two-thirds of the Japanese lived in towns and farm villages and one-third in cities, the proportions are now reversed; two-thirds live in cities over thirty thousand, and it is the biggest cities that have grown and still are growing the most rapidly.

The tremendous industrial growth of Japan in the last decade has attracted more and more villagers and townsmen to the industrial and commercial areas where jobs are available. If this were not enough to cause the population shift, the advances made in scientific farming, commercial fertilizer, and farm machinery have made people's presence at home less necessary. Each year sees a fresh brood of factories dotting the fringes of the already dense industrial areas surrounding Tokyo, Osaka, and Nagoya, and other cities share proportionately in the expansion. Japan has become one of the most intensely urbanized countries in the world.

There are about 600 parish churches in Japan, which makes an average of about one church for every 160,000 people, but they are not distributed perfectly evenly for a number of reasons. The first is that the Japanese obviously do not live in tight clusters of 160,000 people each with a vacant lot in the center for the Church's convenience. There is little meaning in counting in a parish a group of scattered villages beyond a mountain range, whose inhabitants will never see the church or probably even the town where the parish church is located. Parishes are mostly located in the cities, where they are within range of larger numbers of people and where a center of apostolic activity is consequently more effective. A second reason for uneven distribution of parishes is the recent urban shift already mentioned.

The population of Tokyo shrank considerably during the bombings of World War II and even in 1950 had risen only to 5 million. In twelve years it doubled. During this time land became increasingly scarce and expensive, and new parishes did not keep pace with the population increase. The same situation to a lesser degree occurred in most of the big population areas. The result is that there are proportionately fewer churches in the bigger cities than in the smaller ones. Today in Japan a city of 50,000 will probably have a Catholic church, while a city of 150,000 probably has only one also. Only probably, however. In 1956, of 192 cities between 30,000 and 50,000 population, 151 had no church. In the six major cities in Japan with 18.5 million people, there are only 95 parishes or one for every 200,000 people. As one might expect, Tokyo has the thinnest coverage. Although there are 40 parishes in Tokyo, a number far higher than for any other city, there are also 10 million people, or one church for every 250,000 inhabitants.

In effect, the bigger cities are less well covered by parishes. A non-Christian Japanese runs a better chance of getting acquainted with the Church if he lives in a small city of 50,000, rather than in one of the huge metropolitan areas. He will probably have seen the church building or at least know where it is. The Church on its part is better situated to become a part of the life of the city, the priest may become known to a bigger proportion of the residents, and the parish's activities, public relations, and advertising are more likely to penetrate the consciousness of the people.

Yet the best results appear to be in the larger cities. The resident of the larger cities is likely to be less bound by close ties to old traditions, freer in his willingness to examine new things. A relatively cosmopolitan mentality is the type possessed by those among whom the Church has made most headway. If we take the year 1960 as a typical postwar year, we find that there were about 10,000 adult converts in about 600 parishes. Adult baptisms are not an adequate measure of the penetration of the Gospel, but such statistics are the only thing that indicates something more than the imagination of the observer. From 59 towns and villages for which figures have been located, and this is only about half the number, there was a total of 224 adult baptisms reported, an average of a little less than 4 for each parish. This is low, but not surprisingly so. The farmers and villagers of Japan are very conservative, and still live well within the shadow of old traditions. What cultural changes do occur come from the larger cities and they are slow in making any significant change in the pattern of the life lived in small towns and villages. The farmer especially has usually shown immeasurable resistence to Christianity as well as to other new modes of thought and life.

At the other extreme, the 95 parishes in the major cities averaged 30 conversions each, totalling almost 2,800, well over one-fourth of the total for the nation. Of these cities Tokyo parishes had the highest average, just over 40, a figure far higher than the national average of 17 to a parish. The remaining parishes in cities ranging from 30,000 to 600,000 residents averaged about 20 adults baptized during the year, the parishes in the larger of these cities tending to have a few more, but not enough to constitute any notable difference. The only exception to these averages is in the smallest of the cities, near 30,000 in population, which, being marginal, frequently reflect a semirural mentality. It is helpful to know that city limits in Japan are expansive and, especially in the smaller cities, include a generous portion of nearby farm villages. It is not surprising that such a city's mentality would fail to keep pace with that of a city twice its size.

Little emerges from this makeshift inquiry other than that the converts to Catholicism are city people. But it does emphasize the importance of the city in missionary thinking. It is true that many of the parishes in the larger cities would be older and would have more parishioners than churches in smaller cities. But this does not seem as significant as it may at first appear. The first two or three years of a parish's existence are naturally less eventful and less productive, but any great difference vanishes after that. The figures quoted above, of course, include some new parishes in every type of population center. A large parish membership may make a considerable difference, but this is necessarily the result of success rather than the cause, and older parishes are not always very much bigger, as they are regularly divided.

The average parish center of apostolic activity has only a small number of parishioners who can participate in the work. The average parish membership is about 500 people, not all of them adults.

The parish with its resident priest or priests is a parish of the familiar pattern which instructs and guides its parishioners in the usual manner, but it is also a center of activity which is directed toward introducing the surrounding non-Christians to Christian teaching and Christian life, a task that eventually requires a close, even intimate relation between the non-Christian and the Church in order to be completely successful. Such relations are not established suddenly, but are the end result of a slow process of penetration of Christianity into the consciousness and life of the non-Christian, through whatever agency: publicity, public relations, friendship with a Catholic, observation of Church activities, reading or lectures, or a combination of many of these. Not all of these means reach the same number of people or have the same effect. It is necessary to devise means of reaching people who have different degrees of interest in Christianity, whose attitudes toward the Church place them in different categories.

Perhaps we can imagine full Church membership to be the center of a series of concentric circles, each succeeding circle representing a class of non-Christians increasingly remote from the Church. Such a graph would picture, in effect, the penetration of the Gospel.

The circle next to the center, the first, would include those who are both well informed and deeply attracted to the Church and separated from it only by a lack of a personal contact, or some obstacle of time, distance, or conflicting obligation. These are the convinced. The second circle would be those who know little of the Church, but who regard Her favorably and whose interest would intensify if their understanding were deepened. These are the interested. A third circle farther out would be those who have some sort of contact with the Church, a relative or close friend a Catholic, the parents of pagan children who participate in some Church activity. It is a contact which in itself has not necessarily produced any great change in their outlook, but which nonetheless provides a means of reaching them with some portion of the Gospel or offering some experience of the Church and its activities. These are the open. All of these circles are much smaller and contain fewer people that the fourth, the vast outer band of those to whom the Church is largely unknown and totally irrelevant to their own lives. And these are the disinterested.

The primary mission of the Church, in this view, would be to try to direct its activities, beam its teachings or propaganda if you will, toward these different bands of people in an attempt to deepen their knowledge and appreciation of Christianity. These means cannot be used indiscriminately. Little would be gained, for example, if a disinterested person were to be inveigled into attending a class for catechumens. He would not understand what was going on and would probably leave with a worse opinion of Christianity than when he came. The object of course is to move them closer to the center, to aid them to cross the line from unawareness to awareness, from awareness to respect, from respect to desire, and finally from desire to membership. Since the vast majority are far away, immediate membership is very unlikely, but it is no small step in spreading the Gospel if a person crosses from unawareness to awareness, a necessary step in any case for eventual acceptance of Christianity.

The outer band of non-Christians represents a mental state in regard to the Church that is largely a vacuum, not quite a perfect vacuum only because of a smattering of European history vaguely recollected from middle school, one or two passing remarks in conversation touching Christianity, and an occasional mention of Christianity seen in newspapers, usually in relation to Europe. There is the additional possibility, especially if a person is well informed about the local scene, that he knows there is a local Catholic Church and knows its location, knowledge that the mailman, for example, would possess, but such accidental contacts do not give a view of the Church as a Church. It only means that the Church's presence is not a very well-kept secret.

Were nothing done to change the situation of these people in the outer circle, the Church, barring an accident, would probably remain invisible to them. Fortunately, there are things that can and are being done specifically or principally for those who are farthest removed from the Gospel.

Newspaper advertising is one method used to achieve a broad coverage of the city. The type of advertisements used by the Church with newspapers is inserts, separately printed and folded in with the newspaper before distribution. This system has been used as a method of distributing directly explanatory matter, such as a special insert on the true meaning of Christmas at the appropriate season. More commonly, an insert resembling a simple handbill is used to announce a new inquiry class. The big advantage of this type of advertising for a parish is that one can choose a restricted area for coverage, a specific section of town where coverage is desired, without having to pay for advertising for the entire circulation. There are, however, two serious disadvantages. The first is the expense, which although cheap by our standards is still beyond the means of most parishes to indulge in with any regularity. The second and more important one is that there is very little tangible result, and hence the method is difficult to appraise. Few non-Christians can be expected to come to the Church on the strength of advertising alone. Certainly one of the reasons for its comparative ineffectiveness is that nowhere near all of these inserts are read. Because of the prevalence of this kind of advertising—six or eight such handbills may be enclosed in a single issue—one favorite Japanese method of unfolding a newspaper is to open it directly over a wastebasket, and the carefully designed handbill sinks into the depths without a groan, unread, unwanted, and unknown.

Another, more economical and therefore more widely used method of advertising is the poster. Poster advertising in Japan is quite common and the posters tend to be of a standard size. The publishers of the national magazine of the apostolate have issued monthly posters that are simple, appealing, and well planned. Produced for nationwide use, they have no specific reference to the local parish church, nor any specific purpose other than creating and sustaining a general consciousness of the Church's existence, and providing a hint of its purpose in graphic terms. One favorite spot in any town for these posters is the local railroad station, in Japan the most frequented spot, since trains, not cars, are the usual means of travel. There is a small rental fee for using the train station, but it is scarcely beyond the means of any parish. In addition a few other spots in town may be chosen, usually including the Church's outside bulletin board.

In addition to this type of poster are posters that give a moral message, usually an old Japanese proverb, and since both ethics and proverbs are highly regarded by the Japanese as means of teaching children, they have been used in some neighborhoods with general approval. Smaller than the others, they are usually tacked up on any convenient space such as a telephone pole. More recently such moral posters are also given to children who attend the Church's moral classes for non-Christian children and who, it is hoped, put them up at home as a help to good behavior.

A third use of posters is the announcement type for lectures or classes. These, too, are normally placed on poles or in other available space. The effectiveness is again limited, for there is an abundance of signs and poster advertising, which people in large numbers have learned to ignore and, with a large number of children, their life expectancy is very short.

There is another restricting factor in the use of such advertising as inserts, posters, and leaflets, especially if it is at all brash or aggressive. This is that the advertising of religion is distasteful to many Japanese. It not only smacks of commercialism, but is far removed from the mystical, serene atmosphere with which they associate religion. For this reason the use of ads, posters, and handbills is considered vulgar for all but announcement purposes, and should generally be used sparingly and with considerable discretion.

Occasionally a parish may have a display, preferably at the local big department store. In Japan, large department stores reserve a mezzanine or an upper floor as an exhibition hall. It is the usual place for exhibiting local art works or other items of cultural interest. These "galleries" are normally available at very small cost, in keeping with their broadly cultural purpose. This wedding of commerce and culture is perhaps one answer to empty art galleries, for the crowds at Japanese department stores are enormous, and these stores are popular places generally, with restaurants and even an elaborate playground, complete with rides for the kiddies on the roof. The biggest department stores in Tokyo would call for a proportionately elaborate and valuable display, beyond the means of a parish, but the smaller cities are naturally less demanding and exhibits of church vestments and vessels with pictures depicting the activities of the Church have drawn large numbers of interested or at least curious people. Traveling exhibits such as this have been prepared, and are a means of reaching at least the curiosity of many people.

Christmastime offers a further opportunity for a window display. Most department stores in smaller cities are willing to provide a free window for an attractive Nativity scene, since inside they are making fortunes on Christmas shopping, despite the usual ignorance of the meaning of the feast.

Besides advertising in its various forms, public relations constitutes another important means of reaching in some way this huge mass of people who are far from the Church. The techniques in use in Japan are both traditional and modern.

The traditional announcement of one's presence in a community, which is applicable to a new priest, is to make an official visit and leave one's calling card with men in certain official positions. In the parish in a city of 100,000, this could include the mayor or some official at city hall, the police chief, the newspaper editor, the school principal, at least in one's neighborhood. In addition some have made courtesy calls on the heads of other religious groups in the city. One last possible type of call is that to the neighborhood organization. In Japanese cities, neighborhood areas, which may include a population of about 1,500, form a territory within the city called a *machi*. The people within a *machi* form a more or less organized group. There is an elected head, usually a meeting hall for civic and social functions, and the organization may sponsor some social or cultural activities for the benefit of the inhabitants, and work for neighborhood improvement. Some are very active and some are very inactive. In either case it offers an opportunity to greet the head of the *machi* and if requested, he will introduce the priest to some of the neighbors. This is more important than it sounds because, unlike the United States where the neighborhood residents have the responsibility of welcoming a newcomer, in Japan it is the reverse, a newcomer must make himself officially known to the neighborhood residents lest they presume he prefers to ignore them. By taking this opportunity, the Church is in a neighborhood society and, as explained earlier, this makes the Church an insider instead of an outsider.

Besides the traditional methods there are the modern methods, especially relations with the press. There is nothing special about this in Japan except that in a city of 100,000 or so not only is the press willing to cover any unusual activity at the church, but such news is correspondingly a much greater revelation to the readers than it would be in the West. There was a case of a parish party for the old people of the city which was covered by the local newspaper, which published a picture and a covering story. A few days later, a college professor presented himself holding the clipping and said that this was a wonderful thing and that he wanted to join such a Church. He began taking instructions immediately. This man had been an admirer of the Church for some time, but the picture moved him to the Church. Obviously such a reaction is not a common one, but the incident does show that good publicity has the power to bring a person a step closer to membership, in this case providing the necessary contact for a person who is already deeply attracted.

Advertising and public relations, rather than being the sporadic occasion of providing the necessary contact for a person ready to accept Christianity, are rather directed in a long-range attempt to make people aware that the Church exists and something of what it is. By this means some will gradually become possible admirers of the Church, even if they know only a little about it. These means are designed to reach those in the fourth or outside circle.

There are also means aimed at people in the third circle, those already aware of the Church. Several types of activity are sponsored by parishes in Japan which are not directly related to preaching the Gospel, but are designed to establish some kind of contact with non-Christians. English classes, record concerts, choral groups, flower-arranging classes, or any cultural activity one can think of fit into this category. Frequently the people who come have some interest in the Church and are desirous of getting a closer look.

A weekly class in Christian ethics for grade- and middle-school children is a regular feature at most parishes which provides an indirect contact with their families. At some parishes there is a follow up with visits to the parents. Such a personal contact is worth much.

For those in the second circle, who already have a respect for and interest in Christianity and wish to know more, other special occasions at the church, e.g., Christmas, are opportunities for them to be introduced into the religious atmosphere of the Church. Special lectures are also sometimes effective, but the popularity of television has considerably reduced the effectiveness of lectures.

One serious problem accompanying such attempts to deepen the knowledge of Christianity in those who are receptive is the problem of identifying those who are interested. The parish priest has no way of knowing who they are and it is extremely hard for an individual to come forward on his own.

One effective method of contacting these interested people has been a correspondence course. It is usually handled from a parish by having volunteers distribute at each home a postal reply card for the correspondence course together with an explanatory letter. The response seems to average about two percent, though there are wide variations. Since there is no charge, the replies are not all very serious, but most of them seem to express genuine interest.

At certain parishes it has proven so successful that when followed up by a call by a parishioner it has been a major source of new members at the parish inquiry classes, and ultimately of adult converts. One of the most significant facts that this broadcast method has uncovered is the unsuspected number of people who are seriously interested in Christianity. Without some previous contact it is very difficult for an individual Japanese to approach the Church, and correspondence offers a good opportunity to establish such a contact.

The regular parish inquiry classes, regularly three or more a year, are attended by those who already wish to become Christians, those who wish to know more of Christianity and, more rarely, those who have a little interest because of some personal contact. It is these first three circles of people who may respond to an invitation for instruction. The total number of those who are sufficiently informed or interested in Christianity to listen to a six-month series of talks on the Gospel, is not exactly computable, but it is certainly small. It is no more than a minute fraction of those in the outer fringe, in whose consciousness the Church is not present at all.

In summary, mass communications and public-relations efforts are directed to the vast majority who have no real interest; activity groups of a cultural nature are frequently used to establish or deepen contacts with the well-disposed; correspondence courses and special religious activities appeal to the interested; and the inquiry classes tend to draw the deeply interested and the convinced.

In addition to the circles of penetration just described and the parochial means of approach to each group, the geographical location of the city parish can also be looked at as the center of a series of circles which enclose ever widening portions of the residents, relative to the accessibility of the church. It has already been mentioned that parishes in towns and villages are in a comparatively poor position to spread the Gospel very widely. Part of the reason is the difference in mentality between rural and urban people, but part of the reason is that most of the people to be reached live at a great distance from the church.

The parish church as an agency of the apostolate is more than a center from which propaganda is directed. It is also a physical plant with a church building and a resident priest around which the Christian community gathers. The visible presence of the church and the accessibility of its teachers are important factors in making personal contacts, so important for participating in Christian activity and for joining a catechumenate.

The part of town where the church is located is of some importance. Since private automobiles are a rarity, a central location with good transportation facilities is the most advantageous, but such a property is necessarily expensive, often prohibitively so. So it would be more typical to place our hypothetical parish, if it is the only one in town, in an area near the center but not on the noisy main business street. Those who are best situated for direct contacts with the parish church are those living in the same neighborhood or *machi*. This is particularly true if the priest has made his official greetings in the neighborhood and has cultivated close relationships with the neighbors.

The area beyond the immediate neighborhood includes those people living within a ten- or fifteen-minute walking distance from the church. More than the people living beyond this circle, these people will be aware of the church's presence and neither time nor money would be required to come to the church, which is an important factor where public transportation is the usual means of getting around. The non-Christian children who receive religious or moral instruction at the church are mostly from this area and their families, especially their mothers, can often be reached through this means.

For those outside this range some expenditure of money and often considerable expenditure of time must be made to reach the church. A catechumen is expected to make at least two trips to the church weekly: instruction class and Sunday Mass. For this reason the fifteen-minute radius is often a fairly sharp breaking point for accessibility to the church. Outside of this inner circle, the person must pay bus or streetcar fare. For those of only mild interest, for the curious and well-disposed, the extra sacrifice required for travel often proves decisive. It is sometimes noticed that the inquirers who reside more than fifteen minutes from the church often find it difficult or burdensome to continue. A downtown parish naturally tends to escape this difficulty of accessibility since people frequently go downtown for other reasons as well, and the additional factor of the distance of the church from a bus stop may also be important for those in this circle. But generally non-Christians who live beyond walking distance from the church feel that it is too distant, and the proportion of those who persevere is much lower.

In the very outside circle are those who live outside the city proper, or if the church is not in the center of town, who are at the other end of town from it. Here considerable time and considerable expense is required to come to the church, and though this is usually not an important factor for Catholics, it is for others. For those who live in another town or even a distant section of the same city within the parish confines, the practical accessibility of the church shrinks to almost nothing.

There are a number of methods that have been used in attempts to form subcenters within a parish which will make the Church accessible to more people, but none has been fully successful. They all attempt to multiply other centers which can serve as a means of contacting a wider range of people and so escape the territorial limitations consequent on the parish church's location.

The most highly developed form is the mission station. This is particularly common in other towns within the parish limits and usually consists of a building which contains a chapel and hall, but without a resident priest. The advantage of being able to have Sunday Mass, catechetical instructions, and other church activities in another locality is theoretically considerable, but as a matter of fact, with rare exceptions, mission stations have never proved very successful. Having no resident priest they are closed much or most of the time and do not really form a center for a Christian community or Christian action. Although sometimes mission stations have begun promisingly, they quickly become almost static. In Japan, unlike some other mission countries, they have never been an effective means of spreading the Gospel or providing an introduction to Christian life.

Within the city itself there have been numerous attempts to operate a branch of the church on a neighborhood basis. This has been done by attempting instruction classes and activities centered in the *machi* meeting hall or other rented places. These public instruction classes offer the teachings of the Church to those in the area without the difficulties and expenses of travel, but the presentation is only of the teachings of the Church and does not provide experience of the life of the Church. It therefore tends to be a cold intellectual experience rather than a religious one. For the Japanese with their total psychology, this is often bad for the *kimochi* and hence unattractive.

A better feeling prevails in the intimacy of the private home, but of course only acquaintances of the householder are free to come, and it is hardly possible to advertise such a gathering. Although the atmosphere of a home is much better, it is not specifically religious like that of the church, and does not supply a glimpse of Christian life or worship. The personality of the priest, Sister, catechist or layman is the only tangible representation of the church. Usually these home catechumenates and meeting-hall catechumenates are used as contacts, and the attempt is regularly made to get the interested parties to come to the church itself. For even if they continue, area catechumenates away from the church have little power to move people to desire membership in the parish, to which they have never been and whose society is still unknown to them.

The neighborhood groups of Catholics who meet, study, and act as a unit have the one form of area apostolicity that has proved successful at least in some areas. The groups that have proved successful are those that have functioned almost as a parish within a parish, taking charge of funeral and baptismal arrangements for members of their own group, and thus presenting a rather complete picture of what the society of the Church is to those non-Christians who come in contact with it. For as previously mentioned, the inquirer receives his instruction as a member of a Christian group, whose atmosphere, however subtle, is unmistakably felt deeply by the Japanese sensibility, and helps powerfully to form a favorable *kimochi,* always an essential for decision and acceptance.

Wherever the inquirer is able to contact the Church as an active society, the prospects of arousing in him the desire for membership are noticeably better. Any area apostolate built around a Catholic group that quite adequately represents the Church can be expected to have better and more lasting results. Otherwise the area centers tend to be cold and uninhabitable places where Christianity is intellectualized and the apostolate is correspondingly sterile.

With all that can be done to multiply intraparochial centers of the apostolate, they still suffer an irremediable shortcoming—they are not parishes. Not being parish churches, they do not fully represent the Church to those who encounter the Church in this form. First of all, there is no resident priest and this more than anything else constitutes a parish church to the person-oriented Japanese. For a priest is essential for the most important activities of the Church, Baptism, Mass, and the other sacraments which constitute an essential part of Christian life. The priest, in addition, is a trained teacher and presumably a competent expert on Church practice. For this reason, even a foreign missioner whose skill in the Japanese language varies from imperfect to more imperfect, is usually preferred to a Japanese catechist as an instructor in the Gospel, and as an advisor in problems of the Christians. Also the fact that the priest is living a religious life of celibacy, which is highly respected in Japan, is not lost on the Japanese, and the priest becomes an important religious symbol to many.

Since the priest can easily spread himself too thin, most priests concentrate their efforts where they have the most advantages, at the church where one lives, where he is normally available, and where his efforts are usually more fully repaid. Ultimately, then, the parish church is quite limited in the effective range of its apostolic activity.

Japan is dotted with Shinto shrines and Buddhist temples. No village, no neighborhood is without one. There are over 100,000 of each. The Japanese are, consequently, used to having a religious center easily available. Even the new religions have centers scattered everywhere there is a small number of followers. The accessibility of Japanese religious centers is very noticeable. When a religion such as Buddhism has over 100,000 temples, the Church, with her 600 parishes, can hardly expect to reach the same number of people. Until there are churches in every neighborhood, penetrations will necessarily be spotty.

The circles of accessibility do not coincide with the circles of penetration, even roughly. You certainly cannot tell a non-Christian's attitude toward the Church by how far he lives from the nearest parish church. Nevertheless these two circles overlap, and tend to coincide. Those nearest the parish church are likely to know more about the church than those far away. Those living close by are more likely to be attracted to the church through a greater opportunity of personal contacts, while those at a greater distance from a parish church are overwhelmingly uninformed and uninterested; the Church probably has no place in their consciousness. Thus, though any exact identification of the penetration of Christianity and the accessibility of the parish church will never be realized, these two circles tend to merge.

Chapter VI

THE IMAGE OF THE
CHURCH IN JAPAN

The primary difficulty in assessing the public image of the Church in Japan is that it is a small, relatively unknown religious sect. Everyone has heard of Christianity, but to many it is little more than a name. Perhaps we assume too easily that everyone has an opinion of Christianity or that he has taken a stand on it whereas, in fact, he is more likely to think of Christianity much as we might think of Mohammedanism. We have heard of it and may even be aware that there are some Mohammedans in the United States, though instinctively we think of it in connection with a predominantly Mohammedan population. Somewhat in the same way the Japanese, though knowing about the existence of Christianity, does not think of it as a real possibility for himself, but thinks of it in terms of Christian countries, even though he is aware that there are some Christians in Japan.

Just as most of us would naturally compare Mohammedanism, of which we know nothing first hand, with the Christianity with which we are familiar, so too the average Japanese will see Christianity as comparable to Shinto and Buddhism, rather than give it an independent, objective examination. We would probably be struck with the "oddities" of Mohammedanism, those aspects of it that are farthest removed from religion as we know it, and be forced to fall back on some vaguely remembered history textbook reference to recall anything very specific.

The analogy cannot be pushed too far, but the parallel situation of Christianity in Japan is caused by the basic fact that few Japanese have any direct and lasting contact with Christianity, so that, like Mohammedanism in the United States, it is largely an unknown religion.

One factor that is damaging to the image of the Church in Japan is the low opinion of religion in general that is common among the Japanese. First of all religion is not important. Lacking any clear belief in God, many feel that religion is a purely subjective means of countering the blows of the world. It is, as we have already mentioned, commonly held to be for weaklings, and since it is so often surrounded with impossible myths and superstitions, for uneducated weaklings especially. Such common practices as faith healing cannot be expected to raise the opinion of religion, especially among doctors. Having been used as a ceremonial prop to nationalism, a retreat for the world-weary, and a magical means of obtaining whatever one wants, religion in Japan lacks the unified purpose of following God's teaching that it has had in the West. In short, to many it seems tolerable but unnecessary.

Another factor that is generally damaging to the

general outlook on religion is the present lack of intensity in Buddhism and Shinto. Shinto, being a rather primitive religion, has only succeeded in being vibrant when it has been grasped as a tool of nationalism. Serious acceptance of its basic animism is quite difficult for the educated Japanese.

Nor is Buddhism much better off. Although there was a time when Buddhist monasteries were flourishing and its teaching was devoutly followed by many among the upper classes, that day is centuries past. Buddhist monks no longer command the great respect in which they were once held. The monks were originally celibate, until the changes made by Shinran, the twelfth-century founder of the Jōdō Shin sect. He married, and since that time this has been the pattern for Buddhist monks. A few years ago a movie was made of his life. At the climactic moment, he was alternately drawn in the direction of his beloved, then, repentent, he would pick up his discarded prayer beads and turn toward the monastery, halt, throw away the beads again and turn back toward the town. Finally a cherubic smile lit up his face; he picked up the beads and headed toward his beloved's house. The audience was convulsed with laughter, even though the treatment was reverent. There is little doubt that the abandonment of celibacy has lessened the respect paid to the Buddhist monks, a fact that is supported by the remarks of some Catholics who indicated that they were first attracted to the Church by the celibacy of the Catholic clergy.

The position of head monk at many Buddhist temples is hereditary, which does not seem an effective method of maintaining fervor in high places. It is commonly held that many monks no longer believe in Buddhism. One poll actually revealed the fact that 35 percent say they have no faith in Buddha. With or without personal faith the monks chant sutras as requested and perform the funeral obsequies in the traditional manner, the amount of prayer carefully measured in money. The Japanese, though not indignant over this state of affairs, tend to be a bit cynical about it. There is, for example, the irreverent joke about the traditional hand position common to many Buddhist images. One hand is extended with the palm upward, the other forms a ring with the thumb and second finger, much like our O.K. sign; unhappily it is also the Japanese hand signal for money. The symbolism is painfully obvious. Nevertheless, it is not quite fair. The first son has the duty of running the temple, a duty which he cannot easily escape even if he wishes to, as is sometimes the case. Nor are the monks wealthy, and many are driven to seek another job. So it is not too surprising to hear that, according to a survey of students in a Buddhist seminary in answer to the question, "Did you ever think of committing suicide?" 51 percent answered yes.

If the demands on the monks are not notably high, neither are those on the followers. Besides prayers at home in front of the family altar, which are commonly performed by the older people, little is required. Except in times of stress, the temple is never regularly visited, and though pity is enjoined, there are few specific expectations of an ethical nature that are widely disseminated among Buddhists. The demands on believers are minimal, and so make for a weak general practice, which does not noticeably influence their lives. The expectation of a high moral life from a religious person is not the usual outlook in Japan.

It is not only the present state of Japanese religions that forms the background against which Christianity is judged. The nature of such religions as described in an earlier chapter also makes Christianity appear very disconcerting to the Japanese. Christianity, as it is often presented by the Church, takes on harsh outlines to the casual observer. Sometimes a Japanese will brush lightly against the Church only to be repelled, judging the Church to be *katagurushii* or painfully hard. And such a person will naturally disseminate his opinion among his acquaintances. Several things contribute to this impression.

First of all the Church frequently makes unexpected demands, such as study of the truths of the Gospel. There are, hovering about many churches in Japan, many people, especially older women, who like to come to the church to worship on Sunday, but are totally disinterested in studying. They are often willing to become Christians, but not if it means going to school again. Since the study of the catechism is a prerequisite for entry into the Church, this is an unexpected turn of events for a Japanese, who does not associate study with religion. This is certainly one of the reasons why such a large proportion of our converts are young people between the ages of eighteen and twenty-five. Ultimately a thorough knowledge of the Gospel is necessary, but avoidance of an immediate insistence on formal study of the catechism would soften this impression.

Secondly, the Church appears to the outsider under the unattractive light of a body of rules and regulations. In certain areas it is known that Christians forbid drinking and smoking, for some Christian churches have widely propagated these prohibitions. This is often the only thing that anyone remembers. Such nonessentials are remembered as "oddities" and tend to obscure the Gospel itself. So the Catholic law of not eating meat on Friday and compulsory Mass attendance on Sunday strikes the average person as arbitrarily harsh. There was a young man on his way to weekly instructions when his attention was arrested by the sight of a group of revivalists singing hymns in front of a house. On asking a bystander, he learned that this was the house of a local prostitute and that the revivalists were serenading her with hymns, urging her to repent and change her ways. On his arrival at the church he told his story and then asked, with obvious fear and trembling, if he was expected to do this sort of thing. On learning that Catholics were not required to do this, his relief was immeasurable. Such rules and practices, however far removed from the essentials of the Gospels, are nevertheless easily noticeable and, in the general ignorance of Christianity, have a disproportionate effect in forming a general image of what Christianity is.

The relatively high moral life demanded by Christianity, while often a source of admiration, sometimes becomes an objection. It is a rather unusual type of objection, based on a compliment, which declares that Christianity is too good. "Christianity is wonderful— but not for me. I couldn't do it." This is heard over and over again, especially the last phrase. However much the speakers admire a high moral code, which is a great deal, they yet feel unable to subscribe to a way of life, to enter a society whose obligations they feel would be beyond them. Failure in one's obligations is a serious thing to them. Even though we have tended to shunt "Love your enemies" onto the siding of impractical ideals, the Japanese are more likely to face the issue squarely. Similarly, Christian sexual morality, though much admired, often yields the same response, "I couldn't do it." One result of this is that the Church tends to attract the moral elite, those who already live up to a high moral code. While hardly a disadvantage, this still does not make matters easy for the man of average moral strength. He will often admire it, but from a safe distance.

Christian morality is not the only discouraging feature for the average Japanese. The relatively intense religious practices expected of the Christian often strike the Japanese as excessive. Traditionally content with home services of short duration and a yearly trip to the temple or shrine, the Japanese is likely to regard weekly services as too much of something that is good only in moderation. At a home catechumenate one evening, a housewife was reading aloud from the catechism. Her voice began to fade and her eyes grew large with stunned disbelief as she read that her presence was requested at Mass every Sunday. Her rendition of "every" reached new heights of interrogatory suggestion. Yet it was there plain enough, and this rub creates considerable friction. There are family duties, duties toward guests, toward the job, none of which traditionally allow for half a morning off for religious services, certainly not "every" Sunday. But with the growth of Sunday as a day of rest, already true of schools, banks, and offices, the difficulties should eventually lessen considerably.

Such views of the Church as something rather harsh and forbidding are frequently dependent on hearsay and are most common among those people who have little firsthand knowledge of the Church. The high requirements of membership in the Church appear frightening for the individual outside, who, comparing his present environment and associations with Christian ideals, sees the great discrepancy between them. As an individual he does not see how he can stand alone against the world, even if he would like to do so. For these people especially, an actual contact with a Christian group would seem of great advantage, for it would permit him to see that Christians as a group are able to live this life, which he finds hard to believe from just reading the requirements, and that Christians live not in grim severity, but even with joy and freedom.

Though lacking the generality of true common opinion, the opinions one hears voiced by non-Christians who have personal contacts with individual Christians is favorable. Often, indeed, the opinion is so high as to be frightening. One who is thinking of becoming a Catholic is sometimes twitted by his friends as wanting to become a *seijin*, a holy person or saint. For the moral and devotional demands of Catholicism seem to many to be excessive. Nevertheless, there does seem to be a general, if sometimes reluctant admiration for the strict morality and fidelity to devotion practiced by Catholics by those who know them.

This image of the Church as an association of the moral elite is certainly far from the image of the Church in the New Testament. The Gospel is above all the "good news" that man is redeemed by his acceptance of God's love. However unintentionally, the Church often presents Herself to the Japanese as a religious society which is open only to those able to meet Her rigorous demands of study, discipline, ethical standards, and devotional requirements. To the outsider we are often presenting the bad news instead of the good news, for he sees all the obligations without ever catching a glimpse of God as his Father, who forgives and accepts him as His son. Unfortunately, this means that he may never hear the good news of his redemption at all. The responsibility lies on those who preach the message of Christ to make sure that the central element of Christ's redemptive action and man's unmerited acceptance by the Father is not obscured or contradicted by widely publicized demands that are emphasized all out of proportion.

In the Christian community itself there is certainly a more balanced understanding of Christianity and a freer, more joyful life than indicated by the common negative image. But this opportunity of firsthand knowledge is still reserved to comparatively few. Until recently only a very few have had any personal experience with Christianity or its members. Until the close of World War II, the Catholic Church in Japan was limited to about 100,000 members, half of whom were confined to a small area in the south, around Nagasaki, and on some of the small, cruel islands offshore, descendants of the early Christians of three hundred years ago. Victims of a fanatical persecution, they clung with great tenacity to their faith and to those rocky islands, transmitting without the help of priests the doctrines and prayers of the Church, from father to son. They are there yet, and except for vocations to the clergy, and migration of individual families, they still, in traditional isolation, have no great influence on the main part of Japan. The other half of the Catholics were sprinkled over the rest of Japan in small handfuls. The big cities might have one Catholic per thousand people, though this was a greater proportion than the average, and a city of 100,000 might have a single church with a congregation of ten or twenty individuals, of whom so little was known that during World War II some were interrogated as possible spies.

Other Christian denominations, starting from nothing after 1859, had somewhat wider impact in the large cities, especially through the establishment of universities. The educated Japanese, eager to acquaint themselves with the West, learned through this source something of Christianity. But since education, even from the beginning, was not dependent on the Christian universities, but on direct imitations of Western models, Christianity in Japan did not influence the intelligentsia very deeply or for very long. The relatively few churches in existence and their few members were not enough to ensure that a notable proportion of the Japanese could come into direct contact with any form of Christian practice. Nor was this situation appreciably altered by the slow increase in the number of churches, teaching personnel, including Japanese ministers and priests, and Japanese laymen. By the 1930's the churches already felt restrictive measures from the government, and it was not until the defeat of the militaristic government in World War II that Christianity was free to show its face publicly as an apparently permanent if minute part of Japanese life.

Despite the much more rapid growth of Christianity in Japan since 1945, Christians of all sects constitute only slightly more than one-half of one percent of the population, or one out of nearly two hundred, so that the chances of a Japanese having any contact with a Christian community or even any close association with any Christian are still not great. Such contacts are not enough to have created any impression based on firsthand contact that could be safely accepted as the general impression to which nearly everyone subscribes.

In the absence of firsthand knowledge of its Japanese form, the impression persists among many that Christianity is a foreign religion. The objection is not exactly that Christianity did not originate in Japan, for neither did Buddhism, as everyone is aware. The difficulty seems to be that it has never been accepted as the religion of the Japanese. For even though Catholicism was introduced in the sixteenth century, it was also stamped out, or nearly so, within one hundred years. Even when Japan was first opened to the West in 1859, persecutions were still going on, and continued for several more years, even after foreigners were given permission to open churches. It is doubtful whether the suspicion and hostility surrounding Christianity as something dangerously alien has ever entirely disappeared. It will be remembered that during World War II some Japanese Catholics, especially if there was a foreign priest at their parish church, were interrogated by the Japanese police for suspected espionage. The nationalistic tendency of Shinto and the new religions is apparently suspected by some to be shared by Christianity. Objections tend to disappear upon contact with a Japanese Christian community. The presence of the Church in Japan—presence in the sense of a society which one encounters and is therefore conscious of—seems to dispel the vision of Christianity as a foreign phenomenon.

The term *hōken teki* or "feudal," is scarcely less a term of opprobrium in Japan than it is in the West, especially as used by the young. Since feudal times in Japan are no more than a century past, this is equivalent to "old-fashioned." Strict parents are "feudal" and so is the Catholic Church. The opinion springs partly from the fact that the only era of the Church's existence that is treated in history books is the feudal era and partly that the Catholic Church first came to Japan in Japan's feudal era. In fact, the old name for the Catholic Church, still the best-known historical term, is "old teaching," whereas the Protestant churches, which first appeared in the ninteenth century are called "new teaching." With the Japanese penchant for modernity, this is not an advantage for the Catholic Church.

Since personal contacts are still few, the public image of the Church would be derived primarily from other means, of which education is an important one. Public education in Japan does acquaint students with Christ and Christianity as historical facts. Since education is compulsory, everyone has at least been exposed to the existence of Christ and Christianity.

Christ is not only quite well known in Japan, but highly respected for His teachings. Two very widely known quotations in Japan are, "Not by bread alone does man live," and "Love your enemies." This is all that can be presumed to be known of Christ's teachings. Although the Japanese accept the truth of the first of these statements, man's need for spiritual reality, the loving of enemies is considered beautiful as an ideal but, unhappily, impossible in practice.

The Christian churches are frequently mentioned in textbooks on the history of the West. The Roman Catholic Church is covered in dealing with the Middle Ages, with the treatment of the Protestant churches limited to an account of their foundation. Since that is usually the last that is heard of it, the subtle implication is that the Catholic Church disappeared at the time of the Reformation, and the Protestant churches shortly afterward. There is the experience of a Catholic teacher in a public school. One of his students heard that he was a Catholic and did not know quite what to make of it. He told the teacher that after reading his textbook he thought that there were no more Catholics after the Reformation. This incident occurred only a few years ago, and can hardly be considered so remarkable, since a history text in Western countries would be quite similar. But for the Japanese, who have little personal contact with churches, the suspicion exists that they are now moribund, even in the West. A similar historical treatment would be given to the introduction of Catholicism into Japan by St. Francis Xavier in the sixteenth century. Since the government persecutions within the century destroyed the

Church except for the few thousands who were driven underground, once the account of the persecution is concluded, the subject of Christianity is quietly dropped. As a result, it cannot be taken for granted that Christianity is accepted as a living religion, especially in Japan.

A third factor formative of the public image of the Church which has recently come to hold an importantly influential position in Japan, is mass-communications media. In the general run of things, religion is not a news item. No Japanese periodical would, like *Time*, bother about a regular coverage of religious news. It is only an event out of the ordinary that would call forth handling by television, newspapers, or weekly newsmagazines. Exceptions include such events as Christmas, even though in Japan Christmas is almost exclusively a merchandiser's festival and a drinker's contest.

The huge department-store chains must be credited with introducing Christmas to the Japanese. They have lavish displays and decorations in their stores, gaudy artificial Christmas trees surrounded with waltzing "Santa girls." But the Japanese are hardly to be blamed; it is not hard to determine the origin of this presentation of the Nativity. The department stores are being seriously challenged for leadership in the celebration of Christmas by the bars and nightclubs. Since it is a holiday, apparently without meaning, and there is nothing specific to do, wild drinking parties, the wildest of the year, have come to hold an important place in the celebration of Christmas. Perhaps this is not original with the Japanese. At any rate, there is very little in the way of explaining the meaning of Christmas by anybody, though there have been television news shots of Japanese Christians worshipping in church on this occasion.

More important would be the admiration of the pope by the Japanese. Not only the death of a pope and the election of a new one, but statements issued by the popes are sometimes carried in the Japanese press. Especially is the pope revered as being one of the great world leaders, who consistently exhibits his concern and devotion to the cause of peace. Even here, however, little connection is made between the remote pope and the local Catholic church, of whose presence they are largely unconscious if not completely unaware. However immeasurable the results, there is little doubt that the personality and the statements of the popes have contributed heavily to the high opinion in which Christianity is held.

Any summary of the image of the Church among the Japanese is inconclusive because of the relatively large number of Japanese who have no direct contact or experience of it, and of many others who are not notably well informed. Without more than average experience or information it is entirely possible that the person will have no opinion at all. One experienced priest in Japan, who has been engaged in publicity work, maintained a few years ago that 50 percent of the Japanese had never heard of the Catholic Church. It is entirely possible. It is almost certain that if you asked for any distinct impression of the Catholic Church, most people would not have one.

Partly through the favorable but sketchy treatment of Christ in their education, and partly through the efforts of the Protestant Bible organization, the Bible and especially the New Testament is quite a popular book in Japan, though, in common with the Western practice, many more copies are owned than are read. They are for sale at reasonable prices in nearly every bookstore, of which there are many. High school and college students especially, in their desire to be acquainted with Western thought, sometimes buy a New Testament and read at least some of it but, discouraged over their failure to understand, many do not get very far. From 1946 to 1960, the amazing total of 25 million copies have been distributed in Japan.

There is considerably more penetration of Christian thought and Christian belief than the statistics of Church membership would indicate. The Ministry of Education, which includes religions under its jurisdiction, conducted a survey in 1955 which yielded the information, surprising to many, that 2 percent of the Japanese considered themselves Christians. This of course is several times the figure of Church membership. Various attempts have been made to explain the discrepancy, but it is commonly concluded that the Minister of Education does not know how to count. This seems to be less an explanation than a denial of the problem and, given the general reliability of Japanese government statistics, an unconvincing one. There seems no reason to deny that for 2 percent of the Japanese the Christian religion is the only religion they possess.

There is a movement, popular especially in northern Japan, called *Mukyokaishugi*, or no-church-ism. One has only to read the Scriptures, and pray to God;

a church is superfluous. Being by definition unorganized, and its adherents uncountable, it may well influence many more than is suspected. In addition, we should recall the subjective outlook on religion derived from Buddhist traditions, in which a religion is purely spiritual, other worldly, and so not a matter susceptible of organization. Buddhism, as an organized religion, extends its membership to the vast throngs usually credited to it, largely in the form of funerals and expenses for the care of the family graveyard. With the very great reverence Japanese have toward their dead forefathers, this is considered natural. Many families, then, are Buddhist only in the sense that their parents are buried from a temple and that they contribute for the upkeep of the family plot. This in no way would conflict with an internal preference for Christianity. In the end, even if the figure of 2 percent is not accepted, it is certainly true that many consider themselves Christians who are not counted as members by any church, and the public opinion of Christianity is more favorable than Church membership suggests.

In summary, we might say that if the average Japanese does have an idea of the Church, he is likely to have in its favor that he admires Christ and regards the Bible as a spiritual writing worthy of respect, that the pope is a great man, and that Catholics are good people. On the other side, it is a foreign religion, the Church is feudal, too difficult for him and besides, though religion is a good thing, he, personally, does not need it.

The only way for the average Japanese to get an honest and balanced picture of Christianity is through actual close contact with Christians and with the Church over a period of time. Normally, a Japanese can be seriously interested in examining Christianity only through the influence of a friend who is really a Christian. This Christian, if he is a good one, will probably have more influence on the non-Christian's opinion of Christianity and the Church than the few things he has heard. For the further formation of a favorable image of the Church, nothing is as effective as a visit to the church and contact with other Christians.

Christianity does not look its best in print, but in the lives of members of a Christian group, especially if they are gathered together as Christians. If an inquirer were brought to listen and watch a group of Catholics at a meeting or in some charitable or apostolic action, he would be able to appraise what he has heard in human terms. The ability to see what it means to be a true Christian, what Christian living really is, is an important and necessary part of the education of any inquirer. Not only does it mean a fuller presentation of Christianity, but it enables an inquirer to picture Christianity in its human dimensions, rather than as a theory, and this demonstrates for him the life he is considering. Not only does such direct witnessing of a community answer most of the damaging portion of the Church's image, but it is also a necessary basis for a meaningful choice.

part three:

Christianizing Japan

Chapter VII

THE CHURCH AND JAPANESE RELIGIOUS PSYCHOLOGY

There is little doubt that the need for developing a Christian theology of Japanese religious life is of the greatest importance for the growth of Christianity in Japan. For this alone would make it possible for the Japanese to see his person and his life in the light of Christian faith and Christian life.

Having given an account of the Japanese approach to religion and to God, we are in a position to assess how the Church's presentation of Her message to the Japanese takes cognizance of this background. To do so we must examine how the Gospel message is presented to the Japanese; whether it is done in such a way that it can be seen as a fulfillment of their religious desires. It is possible to stress those aspects of Christianity which meet the expectations of the inquirier, to develop them more fully, and to present them as the first introduction to Christianity. For one of the most agonizing difficulties of presenting the Gospel to the Japanese is at the beginning, in giving them a grasp of Christianity that they can comprehend and evaluate. Too often, the inquirer's first reaction, when it is solicited, is not that they do not like what they hear or do not believe it, but that they simply do not understand. The refrain, "Wakarimasen, Wakarimasen" (I don't understand) haunts the dreams of many tired preachers of the Gospel in Japan. Because no orientation into Christianity can be fully successful that ignores the religious predispositions of the listener, it is important to bear in mind those aspects of Christianity which do fulfill these expectations.

The Church and National Consciousness

We have seen in Shinto and even in some of the new religions, the tendency to give religious expression to nationalism in providing a sense of national unity and national purpose. Catholicism on the other hand is certainly not a national religion as these tend to be, even though in some Catholic countries the Faith has been felt as an expression of the nation's identity as a distinct people. This is natural, for it is not surprising that people should feel some connection between their nation and their religion. This identification, however, is only possible in a country where the religion in question is already the religion of the majority.

Christianity is not a national religion but an international one. It is a religion for all men, who are potentially members of the Body of Christ, which is intended to unify the whole human race as the people of God.

This is based not only on the universality of Christ's sacrifice, but on the common identity of all men as children of God. Naturally, this is a part of the presentation of the Gospel message in Japan, and there is little doubt that the Church which exists all over the world and is united under the pope does appeal to the Japanese desire of belonging to a unified whole.

World unity, however, does not necessitate the denial of nationality and there is room for a further development of the theological guidance of a particular nation. Such guidance is nonpolitical, but takes greater cognizance of the differences of national groups, their talents, and their problems. In effect, it would be theological awareness of a national vocation. Such a notion would be similar to the religiously inspired consciousness of an individual vocation, which reaches beyond one's decision as to whether or not one can best fulfill God's will as a laymen or a religious. It extends to the realm of the individual's specific talents, which are recognized as a God-given call to specific tasks like those of a teacher or social worker, an employee in government or mass communications. The individual vocation is felt as a moral obligation to use one's talents and ability to further the purposes of God in this world. But although this emphasis on individual talent is suited perfectly to the Westerner with his strong sense of individuality, it is less adequate to the Japanese, who feel their responsibilities and fulfill their tasks more effectively as a society, as described in Chapter II.

The concept of a particular people which is called to a specific task in the community of nations is similar to the concept of an individual vocation, based as it is on the same awareness that peoples are different, and must live their Christian lives in different contexts, whether that of an individual talent or of a particular culture. There is every indication, such as at the Second Vatican Council, that consideration of the Church in national spheres will continue to increase, which may well lead to an increased theological attention to the vocation of the Church within an individual country. Such a development would be a welcome opportunity for preachers of the Gospel to define for the inquirer how Christianity relates to his national consciousness.

But there is still wide adherence to the practice of presenting Christianity as independent of a national or cultural context with its own needs and aspirations. For even though the Church manifests a growing attention and concern for the national situation in which the Christian must live his life, there is still heavy emphasis on the demands on the person as an individual, ignoring the demands of the Faith on the person as a member of a nation. The Christian demands of membership in a nation form no part of the initial presentation of the Gospel, but are reserved as the matter for later sermons and exhortations, if, in fact, the Catholic is made aware of his obligations to work for the good of the country at all. This is unfortunate, for being an important factor in the conscience of a Japanese, national duties should be presented initially. One refrains from doing so at the risk of misrepresenting the Church by insinuating that the particular needs of the country are beneath consideration. However unintended and lightly administered, this is a staggering blow to the national feelings of the Japanese. Since it is almost certain that the Japanese will instinctively appraise the Church on these grounds of national concern, we need not be surprised that after four hundred years Christianity is still regularly characterized as a "foreign religion" by people who see nothing foreign in television. After all, a national expression of religion is only a matter of defining the Christian's obligations toward his fellow countrymen. The Japanese adult inquirer naturally wishes to know what it means to be a good Christian in terms proximate to his life. With our Western proclivity toward individualism, in teaching Christianity we habitually present obligation almost exclusively in terms of individual morality, and nearly ignore communal responsibility, an area of maximum concern for the Japanese. By withholding the Church's real concern for particular theological guidance of the nation's practices and opportunities, we force the inquirer to decide on the Church's merits without any mention of what may appear to him as a critical issue. For this silence is easily interpreted as indifference, tantamount to ignoring their identity as a people.

The Church in Japan has a role in redeeming the nation. The Christian community must see itself as working for a national policy, a national way of life which is inspired by the Gospel. This is true of areas under the direction of the government, like education and welfare, and in those areas under private control, industrial managment, labor, and family life. The Gospel should be presented in terms which can illuminate and guide these areas of national concern, if the Church is to be seen as having a redemptive mission toward the nation.

The Church and the World of the Spirit

As Shinto has prepared the Japanese to appreciate the religious views of national purpose, Buddhism must be credited with giving the Japanese the taste for rich, symbolic ceremonies of purification and dedication together with a real yearning for contemplation. The ability to appreciate ceremony as a means of expressing an internal change puts the Japanese in an enviable position to appreciate fully the Catholic liturgy, the Mass and the sacraments.

The attraction of the Japanese toward the liturgy is probably most dramatically demonstrated by the non-Catholics who witness Catholic wedding Masses and funeral Masses. Since most Japanese Catholics are converts, young men and women being especially numerous among them, a wedding will often find the vast majority of those in attendance, mostly relatives, to be non-Catholics. Usually they know nothing of Christianity and have never been in a church before. Their reaction to the Catholic wedding Mass is almost always one of appreciation and frequently deeply so. It is not uncommon for a pagan couple to wish to be married at the church.

An even greater attraction is a Catholic funeral. Funerals in Japan have always been important occasions. Considering the especially deep respect they have toward their parents and ancestors, and the reverence with which they hold the departed in memory, it is a deeply moving and meaningful experience for the surviving members of the family to witness their fu-

neral. Although attendance at weddings may be restricted to families, close relatives, and a few friends,
the much larger attendance at funerals testifies to the
importance of this most solemn event. It is both deeply
solemn and deeply meaningful. For just as one becomes
a Buddha by dying and being buried from a Buddhist temple with a beautiful name bestowed on him for
the occasion, so too if one dies a Catholic and is buried
from the church, it is deeply felt that the deceased is
somehow a permanent Catholic. This is a powerful pull
on any surviving members of the family. Coupled with
this is the meaningfulness of the Catholic cermony.
The Catholic funeral with its stress on eternal life—"For
those who have been faithful, O Lord, life is not
ended, but merely changed"—bestows on those in attendance, in this solemn context, a perception of the
Church's teaching on the end of man that hours of
lengthy discussion and explanation seem powerless to
implant. It has often happened that after a funeral, an
individual or even a whole family expresses a desire to
become Catholic.

Given the beauty and significance of the liturgical
prayers in weddings and funerals, it is unfortunate that
more of these are not recited in Japanese rather than in
Latin. For the solemnly attentive people in attendance
are deprived of a rare opportunity to fully savor the
rich significance of these occasions to which they are
ready to respond emotionally.

Instinctive appreciation of the sacraments is also
relatively high among the Japanese. This is true of Baptism and especially of the Holy Eucharist. No Japanese
adult convert is likely to forget the day of his baptism

and of those attending Mass nearly everyone will receive Communion. The convert fits naturally into a sacramental life, though this of course is a benefit reserved to the baptized, and does not reach to an inquirer.

The Japanese have a natural aptitude for contemplative prayer, with which they are already acquainted and which even more than ceremony appears to them as a means of truly living the life of the spirit, a life which they deeply respect. As indicated earlier, the longing to be answered by prayer is the wish for a spiritual self-mastery, the ability to maintain spiritual purity and calm. By disciplined spiritual activity they anticipate some firm grasp of a spiritual reality, giving stability and serenity to a life normally plunged into a bewildering world of uncertain action and certain change. Living as they do in a society that has little room for the individual pursuit of private spiritual goals, the Japanese treasure this acquired tranquillity as both refreshing and vitalizing the spirit. It is here that the individual is free to live his own life of spiritual values and in the pervading aura of emotional calm he tends to regard his religious experience of the quiescent heart as uniquely his own, incommunicable and highly subjective.

Despite the uncertainties of subjective and emotional attitudes toward contemplation, it is one of the deepest expectations from religion among the Japanese. The Church has a long and deep tradition of contemplative prayer, but it has been the practice in the Western Church to consider it too advanced to be the staple fare of the ordinary believer, while in Japan it is otherwise. Rather than presenting initially a system of morality, which they are willing to follow, but which engenders little enthusiasm, it would seem to be wise to present first a serious and solemn view of prayer. This is not an unusual practice in dealing with the Japanese inquirer, and it is a frequently noted fact that when the inquirer begins to pray regularly, he is already well on the way and there is little likelihood that he will turn back.

An important aspect of the Japanese psychology of prayer that is often overlooked is the propensity to conceive of prayer as a state rather than a statement. Westerners become habituated to prayer in the form of statements and petitions, the intention of which is primarily pragmatic. We are likely to value prayer mostly for its efficacy, as a means of getting something we want, and tend to neglect prayer as a valuable experience in itself. Of course, petition, especially in cases of desperation, is well known to the Japanese as well, but many still place a high value on contemplation itself, independent of any measurable benefits to be derived from it. In short, the Japanese tend to regard prayer as an end, whereas we tend to reduce it to a means. This may be independently verified by the fact that by our prayer we expect to get at least some grace as a result, scarcely suspecting that prayer itself is a grace.

Consequently we often present prayer as a duty, not calculated to be appealing. We inform inquirers that one must say his morning and night prayers, and is obligated to prayer at other times as well. All this is true and minimal, but it would seem helpful to present prayer at the beginning as a desirable experience rather than as an onerous duty, for the Japanese expect to find in contemplation an emotional and spiritual satisfaction.

Prayer may also be a way of seeing eternal truths, for it provides a religious atmosphere in the spirit conducive to perceiving spiritual realities. It would seem that the Church's ministers should be prepared to introduce the inquirer directly into such a spiritual realm, for the religious truths he will hear are those of a world whose existence he has scarcely suspected. The eternal truth of God is not just another fact of the familiar world. In entering religion, the inquirer enters a world of ultimate reality beyond the shifting sands in which he walks most of his life. Here, instead of debating the hypothesis of God, he is able to experience the truth of His presence. For it is in such a serene kingdom that the inquirer is able to sense the presence of God, as he passes imperceptibly through the gateway of faith, and experiences the feeling of God's fatherly care and the assurance of being lovingly received. It is by this posture of prayer that he passes beyond the frantic world of trouble and personal failure and enters the timeless realms of God's unchanging and merciful regard. For a Japanese it is in the quiet of his soul that he sees these truths in their eternal splendor if he sees them at all. A glimpse here is worth volumes of explanation. For the Japanese who are willing, even eager, to be guided thus inwardly, it would be commendable to present such truths of faith in the context of contemplation.

Besides being a context of perception or vision, contemplative prayer among the Japanese holds promise of other religious developments they have been taught to expect from religion by the Buddhist sects. Contemplation is not only religious discovery and vision for the inquirer, but sustenance and purification for the believer. To withdraw from the storms of anxieties, petty preoccupations, and nagging obligations which constitute so much of human life, into an emotional and mental calm, permits the spirit to be bathed in the light shining from God. This not only admits the reappearance of the high truths of God, which have become dimmed in the soul by daily trivia, but in the wake of reaffirmed truths of faith, the person is able to rededicate himself to a fuller realization of the Gospel truths in his daily work in the world. To present the Christian religious life in terms of prayer understandable to the Japanese psychology would seem to be effective not only for its greater acceptability, but for an earlier and more complete realization of its full nature.

The Church and Community Consciousness

Since the new religions of Japan have made many people aware of religion as a society, the Church could well exploit further the Japanese social consciousness in presenting the Church to a newcomer. This would enable the inquirer to experience the Christian religion together with a group which is composed of those who are joined to Christ by faith, thus permitting the inquirer to witness Christian life rather than content himself with a mere explanation of it.

Normally the introduction of a Japanese to the Church is by means of a friend who is already a Catho-

lic. He may bring him to Mass and introduce him to the
priest, or may bring him directly to an announced inquiry class in which the teachings of the Church are explained. A distinct second best, but not by any means
rare, is for the individual non-Catholic who sees an ad-
vertisement or is otherwise informed of the existence of
the class, to appear on his own initiative. In either case,
at the beginning, such a class will be composed principally of individuals who are unknown to each other,
and have come together only through a common interest, whose existence was mutually unsuspected. In such
a situation, the inquirer will receive his introduction
to the Church as a lonely individual. Even if he is accompanied by a Catholic friend, he is appealed to as
an individual and must judge the Church on the basis
of the explanation he hears, and reach a decision on his
future life as an isolated individual, unrelated to any
sustaining group. The church is thus presented almost
exclusively as a matter of individual conscience, with
the powerful insinuation that this alone must sustain
his religious life. The first contact with the Church is
limited to the Church's teaching, rarely does it include
an experience of the Church as a community in which
one lives. Rather appealing to the individualistic Westerner, this approach is not only chilling to the Japanese, but places him in a lonely psychological position,
excluding him from any close contact with the society
he is attempting to get to know. One unfortunate result
is that often he is unable to commit himself to a society
of which he still has no experience; all he succeeds in
getting is information.

There are, of course, variations in the pattern of

catechumenates with mitigating factors. One is the home or neighborhood catechumenate, where a small number of inquirers gather at someone's house, usually a Catholic, and are instructed by the priest or catechist who comes from the church. This has enormous advantages at the beginning, for they all know each other and, as one of a group, each individual is relieved of the ache of individuality, painful to the Japanese. In the end, however, it creates problems of its own. Many find it difficult to leave the warm and cozy group, where they are at home with fellow members, to go to the church, where integration into the society is much more difficult.

The central problem is that as an individual, the Japanese finds it difficult to make any serious alterations in his thinking, and especially agonizing to reach a decision involving membership in the society, for he is unsure of what he is committing himself to. The urge to belong is so strong that the act of belief often remains in abeyance until he knows if and how his longing for full membership in the society will be realized. On the other hand, to be in contact with the group, at least as a fringe member, places him in circumstances where his ability to assess the meaning of his membership, together with his natural inclination to align himself with the group, renders an affirmative response much easier and much more likely.

There are ways in which the Gospel has been presented within the context of a Christian society. One instance is the organization of a parish into neighborhood groups which enjoy a high degree of completeness and self-sufficiency. The Catholics living in a spe-

cific area form a small society which meets monthly in
one of the homes. They visit the sick in their group and
even handle funeral arrangements of their members
when they die. More importantly, it is into this quite intimate group that the inquirer is first introduced. With
them, he discusses the Gospel and participates in any
group action they decide on. It has been reported that
the proportion of inquirers so introduced to the Church
who actually joined was many times higher than among
those who came as individuals to public classes at the
church.

There are probably other methods in use which
present the Church and Her message within a situation
which permits Her to be seen as a society as well as a
body of teachings. It seems that the Church as a society
forms an integral part of the introduction to Christianity and as such should form a part of Her presentation
to inquirers. This is not always easy to arrange, which
may account for its relative rarity in the Church's early
contact with inquirers. However, instead of concen-
trating so heavily on getting them to study, it would
seem that the Church's ministers could profitably make
greater efforts toward getting inquirers to worship,
pray, and participate in Christian action with the
Church. The truths of faith are best seen as witnessed
to by the Christian community.

The Church and Atheism

No account of the Church's use of the Japanese religious background would be complete without mention of the Church's difficulty in dealing with Japanese

atheism. We have mentioned that the Japanese mind does not contain even the idea of a creator distinct from the universe and nature. Because of the difficulty the Japanese encounter in a theistic view of the world, investigations by theologians into belief in God and the origin of the universe have a special importance in Japan. Not long after the publication of Teilhard de Chardin's *The Phenomenon of Man*, this book together with some others was enthusiastically adopted by a Catholic group of university students to form the basis of their discussion of the always critical problems of evolution versus creation by God. Theological or philosophical investigations of this nature are important for Japanese missioners. Until theism can be presented as possible and probable, there are a great number of Japanese who seem beyond the range of the Christian message.

But it would be misleading to suppose that a philosophic or scientific apologetic is the most needed approach to the introduction of theism. On the contrary, we tend to rely too much on argumentation as it is. The existence of God to a Japanese is neither purely nor primarily an intellectual problem. God is not an idea, but a person, and it is a mistake to suppose that the Japanese are looking for logical proof of His existence, when they are really looking for signs of His presence.

A purely intellectual approach is rather misleading to the Japanese, since it emphasizes God as a logical necessity rather than as a reality. Such an approach is also singularly unconvincing to the Japanese. Argument or logic appeals only to the mind, and a Japanese will make no decisions based on abstract reasoning alone. They have no trouble following a logical argument, but the acceptance of the conclusion will not depend on the strength of the logic alone, but also on an independent manifestation of the reality whose existence is in question. The reasoning of the teacher may follow ineluctably, but the listening Japanese is looking around for signs of God's presence. Pure argumentation offers no real witness of God.

To a Japanese, the existence of God is less a philosophical position than an assessment of experience. If his experiences offer him no manifestation of God, there is every likelihood that he will suspect God of being a chimera, all logical reasoning to the contrary. It is not unheard of for a Catholic, while speaking to a priest, to confess that he has doubts. When questioned as to their nature, he may say that he does not believe in God's existence, and is truly sorry. What this means is that he feels God has abandoned him, that he is no longer conscious of God's providence in his life. Whatever the bitter disappointment that occasioned this reaction, he feels that he has noticed that God has withdrawn from his life. For him, God no longer exists. When he sees that God's purposes may be different from his own, and gets over his pain, such doubts resolve themselves, especially if the priest can show him how he can re-establish contact with God by trust or prayer.

A theist in Japan is likely to be one who is able to see the hand of God in his life, to see that events in his own life have been a means of God's revelation to him, whether it is his gradual discovery of deeper values, the birth of an aspiration to a higher life, or his meeting with a good Christian or other people who have shown him love and concern. All these are seen as God's unmerited gifts, signs of His redeeming power, freeing him from a meaningless life of self-concern, doomed to disappointment. He should see the place of poverty and suffering as the means by which man is redeemed from his fears and self-interest, an act of redemption and an extension of Christ's redeeming sacrifice. The atheist must usually learn to see his life as a record of God's acts of love for him before God means enough to provoke acceptance and belief.

In summary, the existence of God is not a problem that can be meaningfully disussed in isolation from the subject's experiences with God. For this reason among others, it seems wise to utilize the traditional Japanese approaches to God through symbol, prayer, and the witness of an active religious society. It is through these means that His presence is manifested, by this that Japanese accept His existence.

Despite the overriding necessity for a nonintellectual presentation of Christianity, especially in the first contacts, there is no question of the need, ultimately, of a thorough intellectual grasp of the Church's doctrine. Especially in view of the prevalence of atheism and general religious skepticism, the Catholic requires also an ability to give a reason for the faith that is his.

Chapter VIII
THE ROLE OF SCIENCE AND EXPERIENCE

For a Japanese to adopt a Christian view of the universe and the Christian meaning of human life requires a considerable revolution. We have given some indications of the extent of this required change and shown that the vast majority of the Japanese have not in any way altered their philosophy of life under the faint impact of Christianity in Japan. The change required for acceptance of Christianity is not merely an intellectual one, but one that stimulates the entire personality to adjust to a different world, a far deeper change than we may sometimes imagine "conversion" to be.

Preaching the Gospel ultimately entails assisting in this personal transformation, for until the Gospel can be presented intelligibly and as an acceptable way of life, it cannot be said to have had a fair hearing. The Church's preachers understand the teachings of the Church, and as we have mentioned, have sometimes taken the teachings of the Church to be the whole

Church itself. But the doctrine is not everything, and ultimately it is the whole Church that must be presented understandably and acceptably. But even presuming a perfect catechetical grasp of the Christian message, the problem of preaching it is not solved until the hearers of the Word are getting good reception and not a lot of static.

In preaching the Gospel to those with a different mentality than prevails in the West, the elimination of static is much more difficult than one would suspect. Considering the listener with his different set of concepts, different values, different psychology of assent, and different genesis of acceptance, a detailed, intimate knowledge of the subject's mind is required to move him to a position radically different from the one he already holds. The Gospel can only be presented through the values that he already recognizes, for these are the only means of bringing about the type of deep transformation desired, deep because religion engages a man's deepest commitments.

Many Christians in the West think of their religion largely in terms of legal obligations, which is convenient for those who conceive of law as an absolute, as many Westerners do and have done since the Roman Empire. Other Westerners think of their religion in terms of truth, with the Greeklike vision of truth as an absolute, compelling submission much as law does. But in the Japanese cultural tradition neither law nor truth is an absolute. Since they are sometimes inescapable, one submits at times, but it is not necessary to commit oneself to them. They are sometimes useful and no doubt necessary, but neither law nor truth is considered

especially desirable in itself. It is pointless to insist to
the Japanese that they must obey God's law or that
they have to face the truth, since it is perfectly clear to
them that they do not have to do either. Since this is
an appeal to two absolutes they do not recognize, at
this rate they probably will not either obey or believe.

Naturally, serious attempts are made by every
preacher of the Gospel to make Christianity intelligible
and relevant to the lives of the hearers, but if he does
not know how to involve them as persons in the matters he is treating, or by what means they may be
brought to personal commitment, his attempts will be
largely undirected and their effect diminished by hap-
hazard guesswork.

The degree of accommodation necessary to preach
the Gospel effectively will depend on the tenacity with
which the people cling to their traditional cultural values. For those emerging from an agrarian culture, there
may be considerable willingness to abandon traditional
values in favor of the superior cosmopolitan cultural
values of the West. In such a case, Christianity may
prove acceptable with little or no accommodation to
existing cultural and psychological patterns. The Christian religion may be viewed as the religion of the advanced Westerner whom one is eager to imitate, whose
cultural superiority he envies. Cultural superiority on
the part of the Church and Her ministers is useful and
beneficial at least for a time.

In the late nineteenth century, when Japan was
eagerly adopting foreign things, it was the fashion for
a while for the more advanced Japanese to attend
church on Sunday only because it was a foreign cus-

tom. For a time it was reported that they exhibited a preference for sermons in English. Of course they did not understand any English, neither did they understand Christianity, so perhaps the loss was not too great. At any rate, this sort of fad did not last long, and the reaction against Christianity in succeeding years was very strong when Japanese cultural values in religion reasserted themselves.

There is great danger of reaction when the non-Christian culture discovers that the advantages of the West, its science, technology, management practices and exchange of knowledge, its industry and educational system are detachable from Christianity, and may be obtained without any serious sacrifice of traditional values. However dangerous in the long run, it may temporarily prove unnecessary for the Church to adapt Herself to a cultural pattern that is being abandoned, and at times an accommodation to traditional values may look embarrassing, since they may be mistaken for evidence of backwardness.

The ex-colonial countries, whose nationalism is one of reaction, frequently have a cultural reaction as well. For sooner or later they discover that many Western traditions do not fit their own culture and are not superior to their own.

In such former colonial countries as India and the countries of Africa, this cultural reaction has set in in some ways, and is not usually beneficial to the Church. India discourages missionary work, and will refuse a visa to those who come only to preach the Gospel. For the presentation of Christianity had too often been accompanied by a denial or ignoring of Indian cultural values, and as emerging peoples become more conscious of their values, a Christianity that has ignored them cannot help but appear as a foreign invasion, albeit a spiritual one. Some other lands, Indonesia among them, are notably cool toward Christian evangelization.

In Africa it is dangerous to make any generalizations, but in some former colonies, the Church has been partially identified with the colonial powers and has shared in the hostility of the people toward the West. More importantly, in the long run Christianity does not seem necessary or even contributory to these emerging peoples. If we were to ask ourselves whether or not the leadership of these emerging cultures is moving toward Christianity or away from it, there is little room for optimism.

This reaction is not entirely political, for intellectual and artistic leadership in the new Africa is scarcely favorable to Christianity and is sometimes openly hostile, even on the part of those who are products of Church education. While still colonies, these countries looked up to the West as their only source of improvement, which bathes Christianity in the attractive light of reflected glory. But now that they are moving toward a cosmopolitan culture, Christianity looks to many leaders to be a by-product of colonization that no longer has a native market as it anwers no recognized need. In the long run Christianity must be seen as assuming the values of the culture, clarifying the world the people already know, and illuminating and guiding the lives they must live if it is to retain relevancy in a cosmopolitan culture.

The Asian mission lands of Korea, Taiwan, and Vietnam are currently areas in which the Church is very rapidly growing. But there, too, there is a temporary dependence on Western intervention. Although not legally colonies, their very existence is still dependent on Western power, and there is no reason to suppose that when they become fully self-governing and self-sufficient that these countries too will not reassert native cultural values. If the Church is identified with foreign superiority more than with traditional values, the reaction may seriously impede the Church's progress and even result in lingering antipathy.

In a culture that is already cosmopolitan, as in Japan, the traditional values of the Japanese have found expression in modern dress, in all the external alterations brought about by contact with the cosmopolitan culture of the West. The traditional values remain as vital forces in the lives of the people and of the society. Having made this adjustment in becoming a cosmopolitan culture, which in Japan was already largely accomplished by the Russo-Japanese war, Japan is under no compulsion to abandon its own cultural values. Nor is there any reason to do so. Once traditional values prove adequate to life in the modern world, and once the newly acquired tools prove to be an effective means of pursuing traditional desires, they may be held with greater tenacity. The clearest manifestation of this tendency can be seen in the relatively superficial field of politics. When an agrarian culture under a totalitarian regime begins to adopt a cosmopolitan culture it will often utilize the new advantages of education, technology, and management to pursue traditionally desired goals, increased social control or foreign conquest as in the case of China or Egypt, or preserving the equanimity of moral superiority as in the case of India. Adjustments occur, as some traditional desires like some of the above are revealed as unrealizable, but the deeper commitments of the culture are likely to remain unchanged and merely choose different forms of expression.

There is no pressure that can eradicate basic cultural values since they are identical with the people themselves. The native sensibilities and motive forces which are formed by these values will remain. It is to these deep regions of the human person that one must appeal to show the beauty of the Gospel and move a person to embrace it. The particular sensibilities of a people are the only means a person has of appreciation, of feeling something deeply, as deeply as the Gospel message should be felt. The particular motive forces of a culture are the only means he has of moving to accept and follow the teachings of Christ at a level beyond politics and above mundane considerations. It is to this level that the Church must direct Her message for its full effect in dealing with non-Western cultures. The Church's fidelity to the traditional values of a particular culture is the key to its ultimate and complete Christianization.

Naturally, from the point of view of the Westerner, any such accommodation is unnecessary, since the form in which he normally learns Christianity and thinks of it is already adapted to his own culture. We Westerners often see Christianity through the various facets of our own psychology, a theology which appeals to our intellect, or at least has done so in the past, a morality which appeals to our will for the regulation of social behavior, and forgiveness which appeals to our emotion. When carried to extremes these cultural expressions of Christianity tend to drift off into mere speculation, to harden into law, or to melt into sentiment, none of which is recognizably the Gospel presentation, nor are they expressions possible to a Japanese with his spirit of unity. This way of seeing something or being moved by it is not itself a distortion of the Gospel, but the only way we of a particular cuture are able to understand and follow it. A different culture has its own means of understanding and following.

In our hasty sketch of some leading elements of Japanese culture which are especially relevant to the preaching of the Gospel, we had occasion to describe the Japanese society, religious psychology, psychological unity, church organization, mass communications, and the intellectual world. Each of these fields reveals profound differences between East and West and this indicates the necessity of adjusting the method of the presentation of Christianity to a distinct people. Particularly the emphasis has been to isolate those elements of Japanese culture the consideration of which is essential to communicate the Gospel to the Japanese at the desired depth.

The information presented is actually the result of experience and is, consequently, the common property of all who have attempted to introduce the Church to the Japanese public. As a result, such an inquiry is inevitably studded with tentative generalizations, unsupported by scientifically valid documentation. It is in such a state of shaky cultural orientation, based as it is on nothing more than the inherited experience of trial and error, that the Church is often condemned to pursue its apostolic mission even today. In general, the Church's conduct of its mission proceeds with only the vague guidance of experience.

The limiting factor in presenting Christianity in understandable terms which appeal to the Japanese spirit is the limited extent of our knowledge of these areas which we have dealt with, or more simply, the extent of our ignorance. What sensibilities we regularly trample on are not completely known, what cultural values are needlessly ignored and shunted to the area of irrelevancy remains an unanswered question. Whether or not the Church in its normal appeal leaves great depths of motivating forces untapped is a question no one can answer with the assurance of demonstrable fact. Certain obvious cases occur to nearly everyone, but the fact remains that the approach of the Church to the Japanese people is often guided by nothing other than a hesitant and uncertain experience.

The difficulty of adjusting the preaching of the Gospel to Japanese culture may be imagined to be easily solved by simply consulting the numerous Japanese clergy and hierarchy, who should be able to clear up any and all matters. But on deeper examination the desired clarity, appeal, and motivation of Gospel preaching is not so easily arrived at. We sometimes forget that the enormous efforts made in the West to understand ourselves, conducted through sociological investigation, social psychology, motivational research, and public-opinion polls are necessary because we do not really know what our attitudes are or why and how we are willing to change them. We ourselves are only recently aware of the depth and complexity of human conviction and the genesis of human choice. Nearly all these methods of investigation uncover another way in which traditional patterns of thinking and feeling disrupt what superficially appears to be a simple proposition.

The problem then is that experience is not enough. Simple observation, even over an extended period, deals only with visible phenomena, and the deeper one plunges the more uncertain is the understanding. Experience does not expose the depth of human sensibility and motivation that is the primary concern of the Church's attempt to preach the Gospel. Above all, the specific form of these values as they exist in the spirit of the Japanese is the one indispensable item of information for the agent intent on reaching the person at this depth. This for the most part is an undiscovered country for which he can find no road maps. In practice, the Church's ministers may be forced to fall back on the assumption that the values in the depths of the Japanese soul are identical with his own, which is a disastrous error.

We may discover obvious areas of distaste in our presentation of Christianity, some traditional explanations that fail to illuminate or convince, transplanted practices that will never bloom on Japanese soil. But experience takes one only so far; it only tells you that something is wrong, but not precisely what. The type of information supplied by sheer experience is too uncertain, too disorganized to be a sure guide to adaptation.

Among a group of preachers of the Gospel working

among the same people at the same task there are certainly areas of agreement; just as certainly there are areas of wide disagreement. Whether in the attempt to describe the culture, the individual is describing it, his own reaction to it, one of his dreams, or a mixture of all three can never be settled without critical examination. The inexactitude of personal opinion is boundless. In the end it must be admitted that the voice of experience alone is a trumpet giving off a very uncertain note.

The severe limitations of knowledge about those who are the subjects of the missionary effort, their ways of viewing religion and human life, their religious motivation and means of commitment, mean that the Church's public relations, mass communications, organizations, and instructions are partially conducted in the dark, with only a hope that the particular method chosen for the presentation of the Church's message will be effective. Such modern methods especially depend for their effectiveness on precise knowledge of the subjects. For the parish priest, who must deal with all of these areas, the way in which he must operate is by guesswork, largely arbitrary, with the result that there is a bewildering variety of means of introducing newcomers to the Church. Even experimentation fails to yield precise evaluation, since the priest never knows with certainty what factors may have accounted for a particular success or failure. In the absence of exact knowledge for guidance, the Church finds it extremely difficult to refine the methods of presenting the Gospel and to progress in the methods of the apostolate.

The sciences which seriously investigate matters of human understanding, conviction, and choice within a particular culture seem the essential tools to rescue the missioner from forever stumbling in the dark, but few have a competent grasp of any of them. The sciences which seem capable of supplying valuable guidance would include cultural anthropology especially in religious areas, sociology, especially religious sociology, social psychology, linguistics, and Japanese ways of learning. Each of these disciplines should be able to answer many of the questions which puzzle the Church's ministers and stall Her attempts to spread Christianity in Japan.

A general knowledge of Japanese culture is certainly essential. If it is to be an effective guide of action, such knowledge should be both deep and exact, yielding an illumination that surpasses a general understanding—even of the average Japanese. Specific areas of needed research by cultural anthropologists whose results would prove beneficial to the Japanese Church in pursuit of Her mission are many. A study of personal relationships, how they are established, and how they may be used as a means of influence is one such area of research. This is important, for it is already known that the acceptance of Christianity is nearly always preceded by a personal contact with a Christian. Japanese Catholics will frequently ask the priest, even if he is a foreigner, how they should approach their non-Christian neighbors on religious questions, and frequently the guidance he is able to supply is very little because he knows very little. As with so many other questions nobody knows the answers, and only a serious scientific investigation could uncover the answer. The answer is certainly not a magic formula, but it brings a better understanding which can formulate effective advice.

Similarly, the structure of Japanese societies requires a deeper study. Their formation, their function, the degree of their molding influence are all factors which, if better understood, would help the Church's ministers in their dealings with societies in Japan, not excluding the parish itself. The knowledge of how to establish a functioning society in Japan would be of great value in beginning new parishes and new societies and in reorganizing older ones. Such knowledge should not be confused with the skill acquired by experience, which would come after accurate knowledge, for uninformed experience is a very hit-and-miss affair.

Perhaps of even greater importance is a clearer picture of the Japanese ways of knowing. A thorough grasp of the patterns of Japanese learning and the evolution of judgments is of critical importance in the Church's attempt to spread the understanding of Christianity. Too often we do not know why they do not understand our message or how the message can be made clearer. Misunderstandings, which abound, could certainly be reduced through an application of such knowledge.

The religious psychology of a particular culture is possibly the most important single area of investigation for the guidance of the Church's efforts to convert a people, or to bring them to a more intensive religious life. The question of what people recognize as religion cannot be answered simply by a statement of dogmatic truth. The real problem is how they will give religious expression to these truths in their lives, what ideals can be effectively proposed, and what guidance the Church can provide for the Christian life. A Westerner who feels deeply the Roman love of law will instinctively give an answer couched in legal terms. For him this is an expression of religious fervor. For a Westerner whose cultural values may be formed largely by the ideal of law stemming from the Roman Empire, this is a natural expression and nearly sufficient in itself. But a different culture will have a different religious expression, no less natural to themselves, even though they have the same religion.

In times past it was perhaps exceedingly difficult or even impossible to arrive at an appreciative understanding of cultural differentiation of religious expression. Had it been possible, the history of the world might have been different. But it is possible now, aided by the tools of scientific research, to arrive at an understanding of the religious psychology of the people of Japan and other countries, which may at least prevent tragic reactions against the Church caused by Her unwitting repression of their most treasured instincts.

Besides a deep and accurate understanding of the unchanging cultural values of the people, scientific investigation can reveal the changing face of a cosmopolitan culture to guide the Church in its operations. It must be recalled that a cosmopolitan culture such as Japan's is a changing culture, always showing old values in new forms. Even an adequate grasp of a people's cultural history would not equip one to deal with the modern scene. Besides achieving a recognition of the basic differences in cultural patterns it is also necessary to adapt the external forms of the Church to a changing situation. The necessity of what Pope John called *aggiornamento* applies to the Church all over the world. The dangers involved in change are felt by many, and it is certainly true that unless changes are dictated by a knowledge of the changed reality, they profit nothing.

Changing social realities can only be certainly known through the means of sciences which measure such change. In Japan, such scientific knowledge can recommend the location of the centers of the apostolate, gauge the effect of mass communications, and offer studies of different age groups or social groups to guide the Church's beaming of Her message more effectively. General sociological studies exist in Japan, but nobody else is asking the same questions the Church is asking Herself, and until we use the available means to search out the answers to our own questions, we will probably never know what we wish to know.

Especially is this true of the field of religious psychology. We have as yet only a hazy knowledge of what modern Japanese think of religion in general and of Christianity in particular. If we knew more exactly it would be possible to improve our mass communications and public relations, perhaps considerably. Too often, we are shooting in the dark, unaware of the location of friends and enemies alike. In addition, we certainly need to know a great deal more about what influences form the common attitudes toward the Church. How is a favorable attitude formed? an unfavorable one? Lacking any explicit knowledge, we are not able to control even the impression we are currently giving. Investigation into the motives for a person's joining the Church, the means by which he came into the Church, the difficulties and discouragements he encountered are also things we need to know. A religious sociologist in Japan would be extremely busy for a long time, but the results of his labors would be appreciated by all the Church's ministers who have known perplexity—and they are legion.

Social psychology likewise offers promise of illuminating areas which have always been in darkness. The formation of attitudes in a group, the social conditions of changing opinions, the social conditions preceding choice, if more fully understood, could certainly guide the Church in Her presentation of the Gospel and in Her initiation of persons into membership. With the importance of actual instruction and preaching for the imparting of the Gospel, a serious study of Japanese logic and rhetoric would seem to be necessary. The preacher should know the order of presenting ideas, how to evoke assent, and how to move the hearer to action.

Linguistics provides guidance especially for the foreign missioner, but its value does not stop there. Anyone who has been submitted to any special terminology has certainly learned that there is a world of difference between a technically precise statement and a communication of its meaning. The expert will be precise even when he is speaking to himself, as indeed he often winds up doing, for no one else knows what he is talking about. Quite naturally, the Church has its own terminology, which is not understood beyond its own shadows and not everywhere within them. There is always a danger of the preacher's using a special jargon and so failing really to communicate his meaning. He is merely reading labels in his own storeroom, instead of describing the contents. Nor is the foreigner alone in this difficulty. From how many pulpits can we hear an appeal for a more intense Christian life, couched almost wholly in clichés, which arouses only the yawn of overfamiliarity and underdeveloped meaning? Most people in fact are able to speak gobbledygook flawlessly in their native tongue, whether they wish to or not.

Any further understanding of traditional culture and linguistic expression is of great importance and constitutes a minimal qualification for effective work. The minister so trained will still not know the answers to many of the problems he will encounter that science can solve for him. However thorough the preparation for apostolic work, such preparation supplies only general principles, not final answers, because there is no final situation.

There is need for the Church to employ some scientists in the search for a more thorough understanding of the Japanese missionary situation. Very little has been done in the field so far, for there are few qualified men who have the general knowledge of the Church, Japan, and the missionary work to make such investigations practical. It is to be hoped that this deficiency will be supplied by specialized training of some priests who would be able to devote considerable time to this work. In addition to technically qualified men in the fields mentioned it is also of great importance that the Church and Her ministers be prepared to utilize such knowledge. For this reason it would seem that anyone working in the mission field should be acquainted with the practical aspects of these sciences so that they would be able to appraise and utilize the results of such investigations to the utmost. For even if scientific research uncovers many enlightening facts about mission work in Japan which would make further progress possible, little practical result would ensue without an appreciation of its benefits by those working directly in the field of the apostolate.

It is ultimately the priests working in the parishes who stand to benefit most by these investigations. It is the parishes that form most of the points of contact between the Church and Japan, here that the non-Christian enters the Church if he enters at all. Nowhere is the grasp of Japanese religious mentality or the awareness of various opportunities to reach more people more certainly crucial. The nonspecialist priest is working perseveringly in a parish to pierce the surrounding screen behind which lie the thousands he wishes to reach. At times he may have a sensation similar to banging his head against a stone wall. If there is a wall, only a vastly increased knowledge of his subjects' mentality and of the available means to influence it can demonstrate that it was less a wall of indifference than a wall of ignorance.

This does not pemit us to conclude that science is superior to experience, or even that it is a substitute. Both are necessary. It is when one has a close knowledge of the relevant facts and the practical experience to apply them in one's activities that real progress occurs.

Chapter IX

PARISH MANAGEMENT

One difficulty that has not been met by the missionary Church is that of fully utilizing the findings of social and behavioral sciences in guiding missionary work, making science productive at the grass-roots level. For this purpose, if what we have indicated so far is correct, the need is for the fruits of theological and sociological investigation to be communicated to the working missioner on the parish level and for him to apply it effectively in his work. In examining how this might be done we must first examine the parish as a structure and then see how it might be organized to mobilize its resources more effectively in spreading the Gospel.

The position of the parish as the center of apostolic effort has been increasingly questioned of late. More and more one sees and hears criticism of the parish as an outmoded form, inadequate to the needs of the modern apostolate. It is recognized as the indispensable place of the church building, where Catholics gather for worship and prayer, where the sacraments are received and also, together with the attendant school, the place of the religious instruction of children. But these areas of devotion and basic instruction, so it is said, bear little direct fruit in the apostolic life or action of the adult informed Catholic. It is, the complaint runs, little more than a spiritual gas station and grade school.

It does seem, perhaps, that the parish as it often exists and is operated, cares only for the minimal needs of an intense Catholic life, basic instruction in the faith for school children, weekly worship and opportunities to receive the sacraments for adults. The complaint seems to be that the normal parochial structure does not carry the adult beyond this point. For a deeper understanding of his faith, theological guidance in contemporary intellectual and social matters, and involvement in the modern apostolate, the Catholic layman must look to other organizations. Beyond a certain point, the parish does not intensify Christian living.

What has appeared to some to be the inelasticity of the parochial structure has led many parishioners to look elsewhere for Church guidance in matters that transcend parochial boundaries, interests, and responsibilities. With the recent growth in community and social action of Catholic laymen, the relative inactivity of parish life is sometimes keenly felt. A particular field of the apostolate that has the entire city as its object does not find the individual parish either concerned or competent to deal with it. The territorial limits of the city parish do not coincide with the boundaries of the individual Catholic's life, who though he lives in one neighborhood spends most of his working hours somewhere else, and whose concern for the community embraces the entire city. This often results in the parish's failure to encourage the important aspects of a Catholic's activity, the transformation of the existing society into one inspired by the Gospel principles of justice and love. The role of the layman in the modern world receives from the parish little encouragement, guidance, or opportunity for apostolic action.

Another factor which has tended to decrease parish loyalty is the vastly increased mobility of city people. Whether the automobile is common as in the United States, or public busses and streetcars as in Japan, the effect is that it is often not difficult to go to a church other than one's own, nor is it hard to meet and associate freely with people from different parishes. The increased mobility of people makes them less restricted to the confines of their own parish. Social homogeneity, class identity, and common interests which form social ties do not follow parish boundaries, so the desire for interparochial contact is very high.

Nevertheless, it seems difficult to imagine how the essential functions of the parish could be fulfilled in any other way. The parish still remains the place where a Catholic is baptized, instructed, and married and where he has his children instructed in the Faith. It is also where he worships and is sustained by the sacraments to live a life of grace. If the parish does not grow to unmanageable proportions, it is within this framework that the individual Catholic finds himself a member of a community and receives community support for his Christian life in the world. In addition, it offers the layman at least some contact with priests, and offers the priest the opportunity of assisting the parishioner in his religious life on a personal basis, in sickness, in moments of spiritual crisis, with marriage instructions, and the like. It does not seem that there would be a great deal of Catholic life without these fundamental elements.

In addition to the fundamental teaching and practice of Catholicism which are centered in the parish, the apostolic mission of the Church finds its natural center in parish activity. Although the parish can be bypassed in working for change in social institutions, it remains central in the direct apostolate of introducing non-Christians to the faith and the practice of Christianity. It is at the parish that an inquirer may witness the Church at worship, always an important experience for outsiders, and receive instructions in the Church's teaching. If any direct attempt is made to spread the teachings of the Church among those who have no religion, such efforts are usually centered around the parish. The fulfillment of the Church's apostolic mission seems, in practice, to depend mightily on the parochial efforts along these lines. When the parish is active in inquiry classes and convert work, it is also a center of vital activity which enlists the apostolic spirit of its members.

Also important is that the parish provides the possibility of a Christian community, without which a Christian life of maximum intensity seems scarcely possible for the majority of Catholics. Even though elite, highly informed, independent spirits who have leadership abilities need not rely heavily on such a communal practice to sustain their faith, they yet cannot withdraw from the community if their leadership is going to be exercised and prove fruitful among the Catholics in general. If the parish is small enough to permit the priests to have personal knowledge of the parishioners, such a community may bring great support and encouragement to its members.

But even in the work of the apostolate, the parish is more elastic than it is often imagined to be. There has already been cause to mention the neighborhood groups into which many Japanese parishes are divided, and certainly a neighborhood is a natural area of apostolic action, whether that of directly spreading the teachings of the Gospel or that of working for neighborhood betterment.

Just as it is possible to subdivide the parish unit into the neighborhoods which compose it for effective action by a group, so it is equally possible to have increased cooperation among the parishes within a city to pursue city-wide objectives. Frequently cooperative Catholic schools are run this way as well as specialized groups, such as the CCD training programs and the CFM in some areas of the United States. Youth programs of a city are also regularly under the direction of one of the parish priests. Certainly in most cities there are greater opportunities for unified action of the parishes for community goals than have been exploited, but such cooperation seems to be on the increase.

Even national organizations normally depend on the parishes for their strength in the form of local chapters. Not only fraternal organizations, but associations of lay apostles find their most effective recruiting grounds at the parochial level, where the priest's personal knowledge of his parishioners is of advantage in recommending suitable individuals and interesting them in joining one of these groups. Far from being a deficit in promoting apostolicity, the parish structure is ideal for ensuring maximum participation of Catholics in any missionary endeavor of the Church.

Apparent deficiences of the traditional parish in the modern world would seem to be those of organization rather than that of structure. By basic structure is meant the principle of making one church responsible for all the people within a certain specified territory, that within the parish boundaries. The basic structure of a parish already commits the energies of the parish to promoting the teachings of the Gospel among all the persons within its sphere of competence, to non-Christians as well as to Catholics. The parish is by definition missionary. This sphere of competence has always delineated the purpose of the parish and there are no real basic differences in the position of the Church in the modern world that would call for any serious alterations in this structure.

What often does require change for the modern world is parish organization, the specific means employed to bring the Gospel to every person in the parish territory and to ensure that parishioners are informed on their Christian responsibilities. As the world changes, offering ever new problems and opportunities, the parish organization must change to meet them. The simplest type of parish organization is a simple thing indeed. If we imagine a parish in a village composed exclusively of Catholic peasants whose lives are untouched by the modern world, it is quite clear that little more than the inescapable basic responsibilities

of the parish are required. Besides instructing children
in the rudiments of the Faith, urging attendance at
Sunday Mass, dispensing the sacraments, and from
time to time reminding the parishioners that they
should leave off sinning, there is little more to do. Even
though the Curé of Ars shows how much dedication
and labor are required for such a ministry, little in the
way of complex organization is necessary or even useful.

But this no longer corresponds to reality. If we lo-
cate this rural parish in an underdeveloped mission
country at a safe distance from the major city, we will
find that such a lack of organization may still be tolerable. If the people are non-Christians, it may be sufficient simply to organize a catechumenate. But even this
is a fading image. Within a short time the complexity of
the modern world will have penetrated everywhere
and the agrarian simplicity of life is maintained even
now only at the price of having no voice in the formation of the future.

In the cosmopolitan cultures which replace the
agrarian cultures, the task of the Church becomes as
complex as the society in which it must work and where
its subjects live. Suddenly, the placid agrarian land-
scape is peopled with an uprooted, mobile population,
submitted to an educational indoctrination that has
no room for religion, suffering from a disrupted family
pattern; these people pass their lives in a world where
civic responsibility and social justice are rare virtues,
where traditional patterns of life are exchanged for
chaos, and where it is not easy to be happy or good. Too
much has been written about this already, but the par-

ish is located in this complex cosmopolitan culture and must design organizations which will deal with this situation. Some such organizations exist, but of those that are common in Japan, most are not specifically designed to meet the situation.

In the field of education, there has been increased use of organizations such as the CCD, which has the advantage of a teachers' training program which enables the utilization of otherwise untrained laymen as religion teachers. In the United States this organization is used especially to give religious instructions to Catholic children who are attending public schools. In Japan, the Church's religious education for school children involves a large majority of non-Christian children. A well-organized CCD chapter becomes by this process a powerful instrument for supplying moral training for non-Christians as their parents desire and an opportunity to influence the parents to further examine the Church and Her message. With the tendency of Japanese parents to hand over their children's formation to schools, such a program provides a proportionately greater service than it would in the West. But the effectiveness of this system ultimately relies on an expertly conducted teacher-training system which equips the layman to be a competent teacher. The keystone of such an organization is its ability to make a competent teacher out of an average layman. Nothing is gained by giving an untrained person a textbook and pushing him into a classroom. There is supposed to be a minimum of 60 hours to train a teacher; 30 hours on cathechetics and 30 hours on educational techniques. Such a program cannot be conducted by amateurs with any great success. For such a teacher-training program to be effective it would seem necessary to operate an expert program. Not every parish needs its own, and it is normally possible for several parishes to cooperate.

Mention has already been made of the Japanese Catholic Student Federation which, through its parish chapters, is able to exert apostolic influence on the high schools and colleges as well as to deal directly with the religious education of Catholic students. A rough equivalent in the West would be the Young Christian Students, as they are called in the United States.

In the face of a weakened family structure, the effective CFM in the United States has no exact parallel in Japan. The closest thing to it is the neighborhood groups, but these are not limited to married couples and include all the Catholics within the area. Yet there seems to be a need for some such organization. The opportunities in the way of deepening Christian marriage ideals, of clarifying responsibilities toward the children of the family, of supplying opportunities to discuss family problems, of providing premarital orientation such as Cana Conferences do, and marriage counseling to couples who are in need of outside help are opportunities for the Church to contribute seriously to the strengthening of family life. Preferably, especially in a mission like Japan, attempts should be made to involve non-Christians in these organizations, their activities, and their benefits. To date there is no effective national Catholic organization for family life and each parish is left to deal with these problems as best it can.

The neighborhood associations can be effective for

deepening neighborhood and civic responsibility, exerting their influence to end any injustice or alter any un-Christian pattern of social life which exists around them. Positively, there are abundant activities possible which are of social benefit; the sponsorship of action for youth or old people and services for the sick and poor especially seem areas which would fall within the competence of this kind of group. In Japan, as in parts of Europe, the parish chapters of the JOC have proven both popular and active. This group, which in Japan is composed almost entirely of unmarried young men and women, not only provides some stability to the life which these young people live away from home, but also offers a Christian perspective on such a life and goals of Christian activity intimately related to their lives. A JOC member has, in addition to his job, a mission to work for social justice and social harmony within the workingman's world. Despite the weakness of class consciousness in Japan, the factory worker's environment constitutes a special object of Christian activity, with its own problems and opportunities for increasing the recognition of Christian justice and the dignity of the individual.

In Japan there is usually not a sufficient concentration of Catholics in any one place to permit a wide range of specialized groups devoted to applying Catholic social justice to industry. Yet the opportunity of organizing such specialized groups can be expected to increase in the future.

Because of the small number of Catholics in Japan and the small size of the parishes, it is most effective to organize such specialized groups in such a way that membership in the Church is not a prerequisite for co-operation in the activities. A few leaders who have definite goals and are willing to work for them can accomplish more than a large congregation of Christians who have nothing particular in mind.

Of at least equal importance to the presence of special groups in a parish is the difficult task of coordinating their activities. It is the accomplishment of this that really creates an effectively apostolic parish in modern society. If any one parish is to have many or all of these specialized groups within its organization, the consequences are at first bewildering. Such a parish would seem to have a confusion of goals, which could lead directly toward chaos. At this juncture the harried priest may make one of two choices. He may either resort to complex planning to coordinate the efforts of the different groups, or he may permit each group to operate independently. There is little doubt that the last of these choices is the easiest and may seem to be the natural one. The priests will probably serve as chaplains to these groups and so know what is going on, but once the organization is functioning there may be no close connections between the action of the group and the activity of the parish. It is in such a situation that the parish tends to recede into the background of incompetency in dealing with these groups, while from the parish point of view the groups are simply wandering off, each in its own orbit.

Such an arrangement, however, seems to work great disadvantages for all parties involved. The different groups within the same parish, the same territory, would be working at times at cross-purposes, each with its own pet project, with the result that the over-all action of the Church's apostolate in a single area tends to be a hodgepodge of "good works" or worse yet, "good ideas" that never do work. For it is difficult for a small isolated group to set for itself meaningful and realizable goals, with the result that too often, even with great zeal and good will, these groups have no real identifiable goals, but stumble from meeting to meeting on the strength of an action that barely escapes the classification of trivia. The absence of clearly defined goals is a serious defect, for without such an end in view, interest flags, members get bored, and activity collapses because everyone is conscious of the fact that they are accomplishing nothing, changing nothing.

A parish organization that takes cognizance of all the groups into which active members are divided is able to coordinate the Church's apostolate within a single locality. It is the organization of the parish, not its structure, which often proves inadequate for handling the variety of groups among its members. The inadequacy, when it is present, is that the individual purposes and abilities of the groups form no part in the over-all planning of the parish, if in fact there is any parish planning in the first place. For this, finally, is the real problem.

Serious parish planning seems to be the only effective antidote to the inactivity or chaos from which some parishes and their groups may be suffering. If the basic defined responsibilities of parishes are usually well organized, the same cannot be said indiscriminately of the apostolic activities of the priests and lay groups.

Too often the parish apostolate is left to chance. Even presuming the concern and zeal of the parish priest, a lack of organization is seriously crippling. It sometimes happens that parish planning is conducted by the priests over breakfast coffee. One rubs his hands and says, "Well! What shall we try today?"—which laudable display of enthusiasm is a type of planning that must be regarded as inept.

In Japan, a very high degree of organization is the rule for nearly everything. Japanese simply do not accept contingency in human affairs and have no intention of leaving anything up to chance. Japan is a country where even spontaneous demonstrations are minutely planned.

To get activity started in Japan, long discussions are necessary. These take the form of the famous *sōdan*, which normally begins at a leisurely pace, often with tea drinking and easy conversation to put everyone at his ease and to promote conviviality. As was mentioned previously, everyone has a right to voice his opinion, and whether he utilizes it or not, to feel that he has had a part in the decision reached. Unless a group within the group is strongly opposed, everyone will feel committed to cooperate. Since the Japanese expect decisions from a *sōdan*, they naturally are prepared to reach agreement, and though the time consumed is often considerable, in the end it usually proves the quickest and most efficient means of action.

Meetings or *sōdan* are, of course, not everything. Contacting people about details is also an important element of Japanese organization. As we had occasion to state previously, a member of a society desires to know what exactly is going on and exactly what part he is supposed to play. Not only has he the desire for this information, he feels entitled to it, and often it is the price for full cooperation. Contacting people is called *renraku,* and it is hard to have too much of it. If no one has made *renraku* with you, you are out of it, and the presumption is that your cooperation is unnecessary or undesirable, which slight is not taken lightly.

The love of exact detail is also characteristic of Japanese organizational practice. Nearly everyone carries a small notebook. The JOC members and members of the student groups all come to meetings equipped with these pocket notebooks, into which they carefully inscribe instructions and appointments. The precision of detail prevents the dreaded sense of wondering what one is supposed to do.

The first step in any serious planning for the apostolic activity of a parish is a thorough investigation of the problems and opportunities for missionary work within the parish. Together with this an assessment of all the apostolic resources of the parish is necessary, certainly including all the apostolic groups attached to the parish.

The difficult process of selection of goals occurs immediately, for it is impossible to do everything at once. For this, considerable understanding both of the present desires of the Church and of the present needs of the society are necessary.

It is hard to see how the parish missioner can be expected to remain abreast of sociological changes in Japan or even of theological developments, both in general and as applied to Japan, without some continuing educational process. Probably the most practical form would be a yearly institute lasting a week or two, during which the best available information is presented on recent theological trends and the changing patterns of Japanese society, especially as these bear on the Christianization of Japan. With this understanding the group assembled for the institute, since they are the working missioners, could very well work out general goals for the territory for the coming year.

On the parish level, depending on the city in which the parish is located, important sociological changes may be taking place which could be communicated to the parishioners and then discussed with a parish group as a preliminary to parish planning. It would seem unwise for the priest to make plans on a local level without seriously evaluating the changing scene with parishioners who are both residents of the city and whose occupations and experience give them important viewpoints usually unavailable to the priest.

In the choice of a general goal for the parish it is probably wisest to pick a positive goal which is of some importance, one which embraces the greatest amount of change possible in the three or five years allowed for its completion. Such a goal should intend some real change in the city or in the attitude of the entire population. It is not an apostolic goal if it contemplates change only among the Catholics.

Besides having a positive apostolic nature such a goal should be broad. At this point decision on a narrow specific goal runs the risk of alienating the interest and failing to evoke the enthusiasm of the zealous mem-

bers of the parish who, after all, will have to be depended upon to carry it out.

Once a tentative decision is reached on a general
goal that can be realistically accomplished in a few
years, the priests should meet with groups of the parish
and make the proposal. In Japan, especially, the final
decision should be reached and announced at such a
meeting where everyone is represented, for in this case
it will be a decision in which everyone has had a part
and consequently can be expected to support. The
time and energies of the parish are then committed to
a goal.

At this point, it would seem wise to require each
group to propose an activity for itself which pursues the
parish goal in a specific area in which it is competent
and which is within its ability to accomplish. In this it
seems best to rely on the initiative of the individual
groups rather than on the direction of the priest, for
each special group is better able to assess the possibilities in its own area. No one person can possibly have
the intimate knowledge of the situation and personnel
involved which is required for realistic, detailed planning. At this point priestly dictation has a disconcerting way of floating away in a cloud of innocuous gen-
eralities containing only particles of practical suggestions which never quite reach the ground. Having a
general goal in view the group involved can best estimate what they are willing and able to contribute to its
realization.

At a further meeting the leaders of the individual
groups should be able to propose specific goals for
themselves which they have settled on in their groups.

At such a time, these individual goals can be readjusted if necessary to harmonize with others and be finally settled upon so that parish activity for the next year becomes firmly anchored to specific goals, and each group has a defined part in the over-all plan. In settling on the final form of parish goals it would seem well to allow maximum liberty to each group consistent with the over-all parish goals. A loss of conviction or enthusiasm on the part of the participating groups is a loss not easily made good.

Once the goals are settled, detailed plans can be made out; the over-all parish plan being partly dependent on the individual group plans, it would be the last to be completed. Once all conflicting dates and places have been resolved, a reliable timetable can be drawn up. Then the whole parish can be informed of the apostolic activities of the parish and further help can be enlisted.

It is important to mobilize the entire parish insofar as it is possible, so that everyone has something to contribute, however small. In Japan, the very nature of a society strongly urges such an action. It is no less important to seek assistance from those who are not Christians, not only for the sake of the consequent increase of strength and the broadening of appeal, but in order to present the Church as an open society which welcomes the appearance and cooperation of newcomers, a conclusion that cannot normally be deduced from witnessing most Church activity. Too often the parish appears as a closed society, which ignores the people of good will outside it and operates independently of the community in which it is located.

The parish organization necessary for an effective pursuit of the Church's apostolate is necessary for all parties. The above description was largely given from the point of view of the traditional parish rather than the modern forms of the apostolate, but a change of perspective would not really alter the relationship. Efforts of apostolic groups, sometimes heroic, are often sporadic because there is no definite end in view, so that any accomplishments are transitory and do not seem to alter permanently either society or the Church. It is when the dynamism of modern agencies of the apostolate becomes anchored to the permanency of the parish structure that real progress can be envisaged. Only by serious organizational planning can the parish structure profit from the activities of its most vital members, and the lay apostolate groups contribute in a lasting fashion to the involvement of the whole Church in the modern world.

To accomplish all this requires much more than an appreciation of the problem and general good will toward a solution; it requires above all that the priests possess a competent working knowledge of organization and management skills. If maximum effect is to be derived from the lay apostolate, the parish priests need a grasp of Church administration that embraces the apostolic activities of the Church. Traditionally, parish administration has often been limited to building, finances, and schools, in which the Church's apostolate to the world has little or no part. Too often, Church administration is one of running a "plant" rather than of influencing people and society. In a mission land such as Japan, where the apostolate absorbs a greater proportion of the priest's time and energies, a weak organization of the apostolate leads to serious shortcomings.

In Japan, it will be remembered, administrative practices differ from those in the West. The Church, insofar as it is a society, is seen differently and the structure and operating procedures of any organization is different. What is required on the part of the parish priest in Japan is a thorough understanding of the Japanese pattern of administration of an organization which is interested not in running a plant but in disseminating ideas and changing peoples' lives. The parish priest would be more effective in possessing this knowledge, for the Japanese are not very tolerant of clumsy organization. No less than a study of Japanese religious motivation, a serious scientific study of Japanese organizations of influence would be of great value in equipping the parish priests to operate more effectively, both with the parishioners and with the non-Christian world.

A grasp of administrative practices of an organization of social change suitable for Japan not only promises to unify the parish and its groups in an orderly pursuit of apostolic goals, but would also make room for the utilization of any scientific information available. A priest must work in the fields of public relations, mass communications, religious psychology, and the social factors of the area where the parish is located. The basic principles and newer discoveries in each of these fields must be utilized in the work of the parish if it is to prove as effective as possible. For example, it is difficult to assess how much is lost by public relations which are poorly handled or nonexistent. In

Japan, where it can be assumed that most of the people within the confines of the parish know nothing about the Church, a parish priest who is knowledgeable and skilled in public relations could by this means alone spread an image of the Church that could hardly be matched in any other way. And similarly in other fields. Such knowledge really belongs in parish administration where it is needed.

The mere knowledge of administration of an influence organization of a Japanese pattern does not, of course, ensure effectiveness. As in other areas, experience must be added to science in order to achieve practical skill. When a certain amount of skill in this type of planning and administration is acquired, it does not seem that the parish would prove a handicap to the action of the Church in the modern world; rather the parish would become a dynamic center of the Church's apostolate, designed and directed in order to gradually alter its un-Christian milieu into a society that reflects the ideals of the Gospel.